PERSONS OF CONSEQUENCE

Queen Victoria and her Circle

ENDPAPERS The Queen and some of her immediate family
in the grounds of Osborne House.

OVERLEAF Queen Victoria and the Prince of Wales
by Winterhalter, 1846.

Louis Auchincloss

PERSONS OF CONSEQUENCE

Queen Victoria and her Circle

Random House

New York

For My Son Andrew

Who Shares My Love Of History

Published in the United States by
Random House, Inc., New York, and simultaneously in Canada by Random House
of Canada Limited, Toronto. Originally published in Great Britain by Weidenfeld
and Nicolson.

Library of Congress Cataloging in Publication Data

Auchincloss, Louis.
Persons of Consequence.

Bibliography: p. 201.
Includes index.
1. Victoria, Queen of Great Britain, 1819–1901.
2. Great Britain – Court and courtiers   3. Great Britain – History – Victoria,
1837–1901.   4. Great Britain – Kings and rulers – Biography. 1. Title.
DA554.A92   1979   941.081′092′4   [B]   78–26626
ISBN 0-394-5042-5

Manufactured in Great Britain
98765432
First American Edition

CONTENTS

Victoria's Family Tree

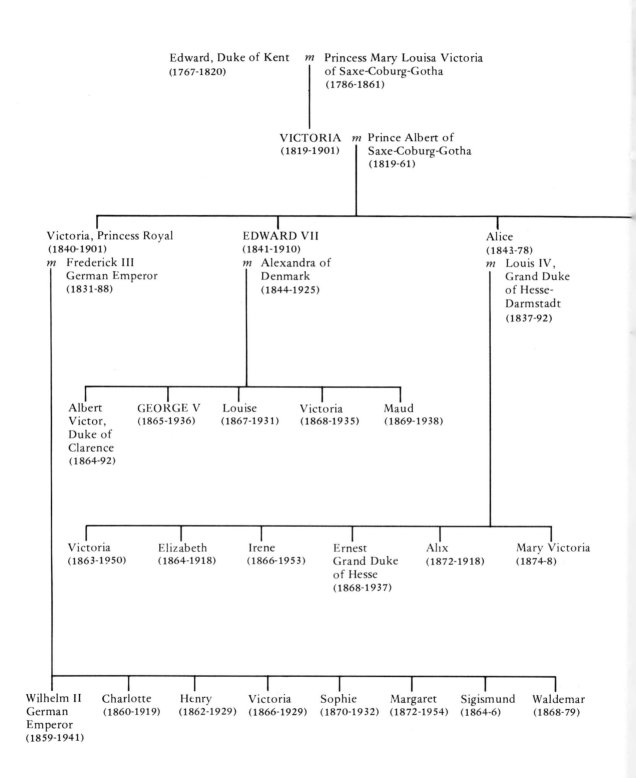

Edward, Duke of Kent (1767-1820) *m* Princess Mary Louisa Victoria of Saxe-Coburg-Gotha (1786-1861)

VICTORIA (1819-1901) *m* Prince Albert of Saxe-Coburg-Gotha (1819-61)

Victoria, Princess Royal (1840-1901) *m* Frederick III German Emperor (1831-88)

EDWARD VII (1841-1910) *m* Alexandra of Denmark (1844-1925)

Alice (1843-78) *m* Louis IV, Grand Duke of Hesse-Darmstadt (1837-92)

Albert Victor, Duke of Clarence (1864-92)

GEORGE V (1865-1936)

Louise (1867-1931)

Victoria (1868-1935)

Maud (1869-1938)

Victoria (1863-1950)

Elizabeth (1864-1918)

Irene (1866-1953)

Ernest Grand Duke of Hesse (1868-1937)

Alix (1872-1918)

Mary Victoria (1874-8)

Wilhelm II German Emperor (1859-1941)

Charlotte (1860-1919)

Henry (1862-1929)

Victoria (1866-1929)

Sophie (1870-1932)

Margaret (1872-1954)

Sigismund (1864-6)

Waldemar (1868-79)

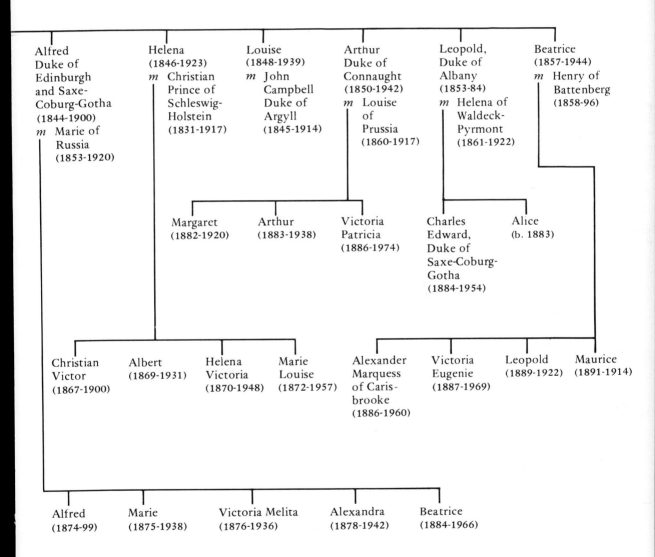

Alfred
Duke of
Edinburgh
and Saxe-
Coburg-Gotha
(1844-1900)
m Marie of
Russia
(1853-1920)

Helena
(1846-1923)
m Christian
Prince of
Schleswig-
Holstein
(1831-1917)

Louise
(1848-1939)
m John
Campbell
Duke of
Argyll
(1845-1914)

Arthur
Duke of
Connaught
(1850-1942)
m Louise
of
Prussia
(1860-1917)

Leopold,
Duke of
Albany
(1853-84)
m Helena of
Waldeck-
Pyrmont
(1861-1922)

Beatrice
(1857-1944)
m Henry of
Battenberg
(1858-96)

Margaret
(1882-1920)

Arthur
(1883-1938)

Victoria
Patricia
(1886-1974)

Charles
Edward,
Duke of
Saxe-Coburg-
Gotha
(1884-1954)

Alice
(b. 1883)

Christian
Victor
(1867-1900)

Albert
(1869-1931)

Helena
Victoria
(1870-1948)

Marie
Louise
(1872-1957)

Alexander
Marquess
of Caris-
brooke
(1886-1960)

Victoria
Eugenie
(1887-1969)

Leopold
(1889-1922)

Maurice
(1891-1914)

Alfred
(1874-99)

Marie
(1875-1938)

Victoria Melita
(1876-1936)

Alexandra
(1878-1942)

Beatrice
(1884-1966)

INTRODUCTION

When Queen Victoria succeeded to the throne in 1837, the sovereign was still possessed of considerable political power. She could dissolve Parliament at will (her uncle, William IV, had done so); she could dismiss Cabinet ministers; she was in control of civil service and Church appointments; she was commander-in-chief of the armed forces, and she had, whenever there was not a majority party in the House of Commons, a wide discretion in the selection of her prime minister. Furthermore, the new queen was by no means inclined to regard these powers as merely theoretical. Throughout much of her long reign she considered them a sacred heritage which she in turn would have to hand on, unimpaired, to her successors.

It was the constant task of the Queen's advisers to see that these powers were exercised only under the advice of her Cabinet. The British Constitution, being unwritten, is even more flexible than the American. From 1837 to 1901 it changed steadily until, by the accession of Edward VII, the principle had been firmly established that the sovereign should be the simple spokesman of the government in power, the outward and visible sign of public authority, a splendid symbol, no more.

Queen Victoria, time and again, strenuously resisted this ineluctable process. She even once reached the point, in the decade following the death of Albert, when her concept of her role was the precise opposite of Parliament's concept of it, where she declined to be a ceremonial figure and sought, in her widowed isolation, to rule. But the times were against her, and she had ultimately the wisdom to perceive that the position offered her under the reinterpreted Constitution was far more splendid than any under the old one. At the age of eighty-one, at the request of her ministers, she crossed the Channel to a country that she disliked and drove through the streets of Dublin to show herself to potentially hostile crowds.

This book is the story of some of her advisers. Nobody, not even Disraeli, ever found the Queen easy to handle, but all

OPPOSITE
'Queen Victoria' by Sir Edwin Landseer. This little sketch shows Victoria in a black velvet habit mounted on Leopold.

A romanticized painting
of Victoria at her
coronation which took
place on 28 June 1838,
by Charles Robert Leslie.

realized the importance of correctly handling her. A constitutional crisis between Crown and Parliament was unthinkable – which meant that it had always to be thought of. Victoria was consistently high-minded, consistently conscientious; she was devoted wholeheartedly to what she deemed the good of her people. But her concept of the British hierarchy was a totally right-wing concept; she was a dedicated Tory imperialist. It was incumbent on those who were close to her – her ministers and secretaries – to keep her in constant touch with the times. On the whole, they succeeded.

Today the problem has been effectively solved. Monarchy operates smoothly and picturesquely. Watching the handsome and charming members of the royal family in the television series *Royal Heritage,* as they show off the treasures of their palaces, one wonders if they are not finer, even rarer, than the beautiful objects which they expose so gracefully to our view. Indeed, they seem an integral part of them. One cannot associate so brutal a thing as power with such perfect clothes, such soft, modulated voices, such stately progress through crowded, bowing chambers. Perhaps it is better that the crown should be worn by a woman. Even in our day of sexual equality a male figurehead might seem weaker than a female.

But although the royal powers are never used, some of them, at least in theory, still exist. It is not impossible that the day should come again when politicians would seek to invoke them. If Britain should ever be split, for example, between Conservatives and Communists, the former might call upon the Crown to save the Constitution. In such an eventuality the sovereign might feel that it was his duty to join again in the fray.

Chapter One

Early Influences:
LOUISE LEHZEN and
LORD MELBOURNE

Many of the influences to which Queen Victoria was subjected as a child were bad enough, but at least she had the luck to lose her father in her first year. Edward, Duke of Kent, fourth son of George III, was so brutal an officer that he had to be relieved of his command at Gibraltar and retired to civilian life. To have been too tough for the British army in the eighteenth century was to have been tough indeed. In Canada he once condemned a soldier to 999 lashes and stood by, with an air of satisfaction, to watch the execution of his sentence. One is happy to relate that the victim, when the ordeal was over, still managed to stagger over to the Duke and snap his fingers under his Hanoverian nose.

In private life the Duke continued to exercise a petty dominance over his unfortunate servants, requiring his staff to parade before him each morning for inspection and filling his house with clocks which struck loudly on the quarter hour. But the Victorians were masters at putting pleasant faces on unpleasant people, and it is probable that Queen Victoria never learned the true character of this terrible martinet. She used to say proudly that she was a 'soldier's daughter' and left directions that at her funeral the casket should be borne on a gun-carriage, which remains the custom of the royal family to this day.

The death of the Princess Charlotte of Wales, only child of the Prince Regent, in 1817 left the aged George III, although the father of twelve living children, without a single legitimate grandchild. There was an immediate scurrying about among the portly and elderly royal sons to discard mistresses of long standing and marry eligible German mediatized princesses. The Duke of Kent, aged fifty-one, did his duty in the dynastic emergency by wedding the thirty-two-year-old sister of Princess Charlotte's husband, Victoria of Saxe-Coburg, dowager Princess of Leiningen, who had already borne two children and was presumably capable of bearing more. And of course she did bear one more, just one, a girl, but that, as matters turned out, was quite enough. The eagerly awaited infant was, in time, to refill the empty nurseries of Windsor with royal heirs and become 'the grandmother of Europe'.

From her birth in 1819 to her accession in 1837, during the reigns of her grandfather and uncles, George IV and William IV, Princess Victoria of Kent was never the heir apparent to the throne, and only in the reign of William IV did she become the heir presumptive. There was always the possibility, after the death of Queen Caroline, that George IV might remarry and have children, and Adelaide, the consort of William IV did not in his lifetime exceed the childbearing age. She did, in fact, bear two daughters, one of whom lived for several months, and there was even an ill-founded rumour that she was pregnant at the time of her husband's death. In addition to these dynastic threats to Victoria's succession, there was also the possibility, however remote, that adherents of the Duke of Cumberland, Kent's next younger brother, might raise the cry that an extension of the Salic law (barring succession of females) from Germany to England would save Hanover from being lost to the British Crown, as indeed it was when William IV died. But few Englishmen cared about Hanover, which would have only been a headache, anyway, at the time of the German unification. Most people were confident that the little Kent princess would one day be their queen.

The widowed Duchess of Kent had complete control over the royal infant with this great destiny. Nobody was more aware of the dangers to her dreams in the amativeness of her brothers-in-law and in the sinister character of Cumberland, but she knew that the odds were on her side, and she seemed to believe that she could actually improve them by loudly and constantly blowing her own horn. The more she was snubbed by the royal family, or the more her requests for raises in her allowance were refused, or the more she was threatened with the removal of Victoria from her custody, by so much more did she enlarge her claims for precedence and parade about the country exhibiting her infant to the great families as their future monarch. The Duchess's arrogance and bad temper, her endless suspicions and constant screaming about her rights made her unpopular with everyone and offered to the grave, silent, all-observing little girl, so constantly at her side, the first never-to-be-forgotten lesson about how royalty should *not* behave.

The Duchess, although not an unattractive woman in her younger days, had grown hard and bossy in middle age. Her lot,

to be sure, was not an easy one. She found herself alone and almost friendless in a strange, hostile country. It was perhaps understandable that she should have fallen prey to the glib, vulgar Irishman, Sir John Conroy, who became the superintendent of her household, perhaps her lover, and who plundered her small treasury. But with a little softness, a modicum of charm, the Duchess could have found any number of friends in high places. She was one of those who prefer to do things the hard way, who actually enjoy the sensation of making a bad impression, who would risk a lifetime's ambition for the satisfaction of making one effectively disagreeable remark.

She was not a good mother. Certainly she treated Feodora, her daughter by Leiningen, harshly and coldly. But then Feodora was of no importance to her except for the brief, dangerous moment when she attracted the ogling attention of old George IV. The Duchess had made her plans to be mother of a subservient queen regnant, not of a resentful queen consort! Feodora was sent packing to Germany to join her brother Charles, and the Duchess was able to devote her undivided attention to Victoria.

The child was reared in a kind of cocoon of maternal supervision. She slept in her mother's bedroom. She saw few other children but Conroy's daughters. She was educated entirely by tutors and governesses, who came to Kensington Palace. It was the Duchess's plan to *own* Victoria; they would share life, and they would share Britain. The future queen was to make up to

16

her mother for everything: the loss of husbands, of native land, the coldness of foreigners, the exiguity of income. In later life Victoria used to wonder ruefully if she had not been unfair to her mother. But she had not been. The Duchess's love was only a rabid possessiveness. Her and Conroy's violent and unsuccessful effort to induce the Princess to sign a document declaring that she would need a regent, even if she were of age when she succeeded, is ample proof of this.

But there was a loophole to their schemes. The person who helped the little Princess to preserve her individuality and equanimity in this guarded Byzantine cloister was her governess, Louise Lehzen. She was a Hanoverian and had been created a baroness of that kingdom by George IV. She remains a shadowy character in history and has been the sport of many writers, from Lytton Strachey, who has immortalized her passion for caraway seeds, which she sprinkled on her bread and butter, her cabbage and even her roast beef, to Daphne Bennett, who goes so far as to suggest that she twice planned to murder Prince Albert. And in dramas, of course, she plays the role of the poor relic of the Queen's virginal years, discarded, like an old Raggedy Ann doll, with the advent of the hero and passion. But I suggest that she performed a vital role in Victoria's story, and one for which neither her mistress nor history has given her adequate credit.

For what Lehzen gave to the young Victoria was what the child

BELOW LEFT Sir John Conroy, superintendent of the Duchess of Kent's household, who, with his mistress, tried unsuccessfully to manipulate the young Victoria.

BELOW RIGHT 'Princess Feodora of Hohenlohe-Langenburg' by John Phillip. Feodora was Victoria's half-sister and their relationship was always affectionate.

otherwise would have altogether lacked and desperately missed: a total love and devotion. I have not read any commentator who suggests that she had, even after her pupil's accession, the smallest interest in rank, wealth, or political power. She was later to enjoy her position at Court as the Queen's domestic secretary. Why not? She liked to bustle about and give orders. But this was the natural self-importance of the amanuensis; basically she had reduced herself to a mere aspect of the royal personality. And for the lonely child with the cold, bossy mother and the little court of sycophants, it must have meant all the world to have a friend who lived for her alone. Had Lehzen been a weak person, she would still have made a great gift to her pupil in her love, but she was not weak. She was strong, and Victoria, for all her devotion to her governess, was a little bit in awe of her. Lehzen taught her to control her moods and tantrums. Lehzen taught her to wear a mask of dignity in a potentially dangerous world.

When Victoria became queen, she acted with a firmness and a clarity of purpose that astonished the world. The first thing that she did was to separate herself from her mother. The bedroom, always shared by the two, would never be shared again. Conroy was banished from her presence. The title of 'Queen Mother', ridiculously requested by the Duchess, was curtly refused. The Duchess shrieked to all and sundry that she had become 'nothing', but she raved in vain. The silent little girl, who had always obeyed 'Mama', proved overnight to be a dominating mistress.

The Duchess had little doubt from what quarter the blow had fallen. She had simply and fatally (for her own plans) underestimated the governess's influence. For years Lehzen had formed a tiny court within a court. Conroy and the Duchess would have long ago sent her packing, like Feodora, but for the protection of the royal family, who saw in Lehzen a desirable counterbalancing force. But the Duchess, in her defeat, blamed Lehzen too much for what had happened. The person who had really reduced her dream to such a shambles was her own all-seeing and all-noting little daughter. Lehzen had not created that ineluctable will-power; she had simply guarded its possessor in her tender years and kept it from being crushed.

Victoria as a girl (and always thereafter) kept a diary. One feels in it the constant presence of the governess. There is much exchange of presents on Victoria's birthdays. Lehzen gives her

for her thirteenth a 'lovely music book' and receives in return 'a little white and gold pincushion and a pin with two little gold hearts hanging to it'. Another year Lehzen gives her 'a pretty little china figure and a lovely little china basket' and receives a 'golden chain'. Once again Lehzen gives her 'a lovely little leather box with knives, pencils, etc. in it, two small dictionaries and a very pretty print of Mdlle. Taglioni'. And so it goes. Everything is precisely noted. Of course, we know that Lehzen read the journal, but it was never in Victoria's nature to flatter. Had she disliked Lehzen or Lehzen's presents, she would have been silent.

There is a marked difference in the diary's references to Lehzen and to 'Mama'. The notes about the latter are clear and dutiful, but the interlineations convey a more spontaneous feeling for the governess: 'I must not omit to mention how very anxious my dear Mama was throughout my indisposition, and how unceasing *dear* Lehzen was in her attentions and care to me...'

Victoria's sketch of her governess, Louise, Baroness Lehzen, done on 30 November 1833. Lehzen gave her pupil what she lacked – total love and devotion.

19

The distinction seems to be that the Duchess is to be revered for the heavy weight of her own troubles, to which a daughter's illness simply provides an additional burden, but Lehzen, who is too selfless to have troubles of her own, is to be loved for giving her all to the diarist. Here is the mood in which Victoria goes to her confirmation: 'I went with the firm determination to become a true Christian, to try and comfort my dear Mama in all her griefs, trials and anxieties, and to become a true and affectionate daughter to her. Also to be obedient to *dear* Lehzen who has done so much for me.'

In the November of 1835, at the age of sixteen, the Princess records this ultimate tribute to her friend:

Dear good Lehzen takes such care of me, and is so unceasing in her attentions to me, that I shall never be able to repay her sufficiently for it but by my love and gratitude. I never can sufficiently repay her for all she has *borne* and done for me. She is the *most affectionate, devoted, attached* and *disinterested* friend I have, and I love her most dearly...

The diary might almost be written in a cipher to warn us about 'Mama'. For who else is it who is *not* devoted, *not* disinterested? The most important and consistent trait of Victoria's character throughout her whole life was her absolute honesty. She could never misrepresent a fact. One can make out what she feels about her mother only by what she does *not* say. Lehzen herself was witness to her pupil's veracity. The Queen quotes her proudly:

I told Lord Melbourne that though Lehzen had often said that she had *never* seen such a passionate and naughty child as I was, still that I had never told a falsehood, though I knew I would be punished; Lord Melbourne said: 'That is a fine character,' and I added that Lehzen entrusted me with things which I knew she would not like me to tell again, and that when I was ever so naughty, I never threatened to tell, or ever did tell them.

Lehzen's congeniality was not only in the support that she offered against the Duchess and Conroy; she ushered the Princess into intellectual gardens unfrequented by that philistine pair. Lehzen appears to have been a great admirer of French literature; she and the Princess read aloud the tragedies of Racine, the memoirs of Sully, the letters of Madame de Sévigné. The latter was a particular favourite with Victoria; she speaks of herself and Lehzen now being 'in the middle of the tenth volume'. When Lord Melbourne let fall the remark: 'No woman ever wrote a really good book,' he was immediately forced to make an exception for the great marquise.

Victoria was considerably more cultivated than some of her biographers have allowed. She spoke perfect German, excellent French and adequate Italian; she was well read in literature and history; she sketched charmingly, and she had a trained ear for music. Because as queen she was uncomfortable in the company of scientists of whose fields she was ignorant, it is sometimes assumed that she was less well educated than she was. But few men of her era, let alone women, received any training at all in the sciences. Victoria was almost a blue stocking by modern standards, and Lehzen deserves much of the credit. We even catch a glimpse of Lehzen immersed in Blackstone because the Queen had asked her if the sovereign's consent was always required for a marriage in the royal family.

The moment that must have been the proudest of Lehzen's life was that in the coronation when her former pupil, in all her glory, acknowledged her presence in the Abbey. Here is how the Queen records it:

I descended from the throne and went into St Edward's Chapel with my Ladies, Train-bearers and Lord Willoughby, where I took off the Dalmatic robe, Supertunica, and put on the Purple Velvet Kirtle and Mantle, and proceeded again to the throne, which I ascended leaning on Lord Melbourne's hand. There was another present at this ceremony, in the box immediately above the Royal Box, and who witnessed all; it was Lehzen, whose eye I caught when on the throne, and we exchanged smiles.

The marriage of Queen Victoria and Prince Albert in the Chapel Royal, St James's Palace. Painting by George Hayter.

There seems to be no direct evidence of how Lehzen exercised her influence on her pupil. It is all surmise. But it is difficult to believe that a girl of eighteen should, immediately upon her accession to the crown, so calmly and firmly have relegated to a subsidiary and humiliating dependency the mother who up to that moment had exercised an unchallenged and despotic control over her, unless she had had a friend and ally to help her plan the *coup*. Let us also note that when the Duchess of Kent was banished from her daughter's bedroom and granted audiences only by appointment, Lehzen was moved into the chamber directly adjoining the Queen's with constant access to her mistress.

I suspect that the Princess discussed long and passionately with her one trusted friend the manœuvres of her mother and Conroy. I have little doubt that Lehzen helped to strengthen her resistance in her refusal to request an extension of the regency beyond her nineteenth year and to appoint the dreadful Conroy as her private secretary. It was probably not necessary for Lehzen to tell her pupil what to do. Her role may have been simply to keep constantly before her mind the vision of the power that would be hers when the old King died. The moment the breath was out of that rotund body, the impregnable citadel of the Duchess and Conroy, in which the little Princess had been so tightly immured, would disappear as with the tap of a good fairy's wand in a children's tale.

Lehzen's role was largely completed with her pupil's accession. Thereafter, she was simply the Queen's old nurse, dignified to the position of domestic secretary. She was constantly present, to be sure, for the Queen loved her and clung to her, but there is not a shred of evidence that she tried to exercise, or even desired to exercise, the smallest political influence. She was 'family', a person to relax with at the end of the day, to tell one's intimate thoughts and impressions to, a comforting relic of childhood, a sort of teddy bear to hug.

Lord Melbourne, the Queen's first Prime Minister, had the good sense to see that Lehzen was no threat at all to him and took pains to make her his devoted friend. We can picture him, greeting her genially, as she is about to slip away before his session with the Queen, complimenting her on her dress, raising his hands at the magnitude of her palace tasks, perhaps thanking his 'lucky star' that he is only a prime minister, while Lehzen, blushing, curtseying, enchanted, disappears from the room and from his mind. Albert, four years later, was to be less fortunate. Lehzen would not disappear from the scenes that *he* haunted. He would find her performing the tasks of a queen consort and managing to imply that the husband of a queen regnant was a useless thing! What a prime minister would not even have to notice, a husband would not be able to endure. Albert would have to send her away.

The Duchess of Kent in later years resigned herself to political powerlessness and sensibly concluded that her own role in British society was limited to being mother of the sovereign and grand-mother of the royal children. She became relaxed, even amiable, a dear old affectionate German grandmamma. Albert, her nephew as well as her son-in-law, liked and respected her; Victoria followed his example. All was made up between them. Poor Lehzen was sacrificed a second time on the fire of their reconciliation. When the Duchess died, a few months before Albert, and the Queen read in her papers how constantly her thoughts had dwelt on her darling daughter, she decided that Lehzen, even if her motives had been good, had caused needless friction between them. Exiled from her presence, Lehzen was now exiled from her heart.

Strachey describes the governess's removal in a telling sentence: 'Returning to her native Hanover she established herself at Buckeburg in a small but comfortable house, the walls of which were entirely covered by portraits of Her Majesty.' She received letters, from time to time, from her former pupil, but that was all. The Queen's last will and testament, dated 25 October 1897, long after Lehzen's death, contains the following preamble about those who have gone before her:

I die in peace with all fully aware of my many faults relying with confidence on the love, mercy and goodness of my Heavenly Father and His Blessed Son & earnestly trusting to be reunited to my beloved Husband, my dearest Mother, my beloved Children and 3 dear sons-in-law. – And all who have been very near & dear to me on earth.

Also I hope to meet those who have so faithfully & so devotedly served me especially good John Brown and good Annie Macdonald who I trusted would help to lay my remains in my coffin & to see me placed next to my dearly loved Husband in the mausoleum at Frogmore.

One notes the hierarchical propriety. The servants, even the beloved gillie, Brown, must wait for the second paragraph. But Lehzen is not mentioned at all.

There must be few figures in English political history about whom there is such unanimity of opinion as that quintessence of the Whig aristocrat, William Lamb, second Viscount Melbourne. David Cecil has expressed this synthesis of views in an admirable biography which recreates vividly the charm of this dedicated amateur in the business of good living. Melbourne was humane, witty, shrewd, realistic to the point of cynicism, and firmly convinced that very little could be done to change the ways of men. 'I am not a subscribing sort of fellow,' he would say to seekers of charitable contributions. He liked, rather lazily, to watch the passing scene and to direct it, ever so slightly, whenever

'Queen Victoria with Lord Melbourne, the Marquess of Conyngham and others' by Sir Francis Grant. Victoria's spaniel Dash runs in the foreground.

24

there seemed to be a snag. We all know that he preferred the Order of the Garter because there was no merit in it and that he believed that nobody did anything very foolish except from some strong principle. It is a common metaphor to liken him and his eager pupil, the young Queen, to the tired old dying eighteenth century and the passionate young nineteenth. 'This damn morality will ruin everything,' he used to grumble.

But it is one thing for a man to espouse such principles in private life and another for him to do so when he elects, quite of his own accord, to go into the business of governing his fellow men. Then he subjects himself to an examination of what he has done for them. It ceases to be simply amusing when the man at the helm of state professes to care only for what is 'tranquil and stable' and tosses away such a novel as *Oliver Twist* because it deals with 'workhouses and pickpockets'. And how would a black man on a Jamaica plantation, toiling eighteen hours a day, react to this retort to Archbishop Whatley? 'I say, Archbishop, what do you think I would have done about this slavery business if I had my own way? I would have done nothing at all. It is all a pack of nonsense. There always have been slaves in most civilized countries. However, they would have their own way, and we have abolished slavery. But it is all great folly.'

And how would a person who had spent his childhood in a dark factory in Liverpool feel about this entry in the Queen's diary?

He doubts education will ever do any good; says, all Government has to do 'is to prevent and punish crime, and to preserve contracts'. He is FOR labour and does not think the factory children are too much worked; and thinks it very wrong that parents should not be allowed to send their children who are under a certain age, to work. He said to Miss Murray, 'If you'd only have the goodness to leave them alone,' which made us laugh; we asked did *he* derive no benefit from education? 'I derived no morality from it,' he replied funnily; 'that I derived at an earlier date.'

Some of the charm begins to fade.

Melbourne, the aristocrat, did not know the name of his own great-grandfather in the male line. The Lambs came up through the bar and married fortunes. William, second son of the first Viscount Melbourne, was trained for the bar, but his elder brother's death removed the necessity of his having to earn a living. His marriage to the beautiful and tempestuous Lady Caroline Ponsonby was ruined by her temperament, which bordered on insanity. Her notorious affair with Byron, her many infidelities, made her the scandal of London, but her ever-forgiving husband could never repudiate her. Caroline, for all her follies, adored her handsome William, and he was too soft-hearted to reject anyone who leaned on him. After her death, leaving him with a single child, an idiot son, he had no occupation in life but his books, his sports – and politics.

Never has a politician gone further, with less pushing of himself. Melbourne became Whig Prime Minister under William IV largely because so many members of Parliament liked and trusted him. He represented moderate liberal opinion only insofar as he advocated reform of electoral qualifications to the extent necessary to avoid open revolution. Aside from this, he favoured the *status quo* in everything; in economics, in education, in welfare, in social life. He was dedicated to the proposition that any change was apt to be a change for the worse.

When Victoria succeeded, he was fifty-eight years of age, but already physically an old man. The idea of guiding a young, eager and idealistic female sovereign in the first years of her reign appealed immensely to him. It appealed to him as a frustrated father, as a patriotic and gallant British gentleman, as a curious observer of the human scene and, last but not least, as a statesman who knew that he had never realized his full potential and saw in this assignment the possibility of at last doing one great thing.

The Queen had never had a father, or even, as we have seen, much of a mother; she had not yet fallen in love or, except for the discreet Lehzen, had an intimate friend. She found in this charming, kindly, cultivated, witty and still handsome elderly man a combination of parent, swain and tutor. She wanted to know his opinion about everything that concerned herself: about her family, her forebears, her mother, her dogs, her entertainments, the hours she should keep, the people she should see, and, of course, whom and when she should marry. Her curiosity about his own life, too, was inexhaustible: she questioned him about his marriage to the point of tactlessness, about his schools, his habits, his health, his friends, his religious beliefs and *why* he seemed to prefer to dine with Lady Holland than with his sovereign. And every night she carefully inscribed his answers and comments in her faithfully kept journal. Melbourne was thus preserved for posterity; what other man has had his sovereign for a Boswell?

It is a charming picture: the young Queen and the old Minister seated together on a divan turning the pages of those volumes of historical portraits so popular at the time: Melbourne telling anecdotes about the personalities of those depicted, filling in the dry pages of his pupil's historical education with lively vignettes of old-time kings and queens, of statesmen and warriors and great beauties, of murders and passions and violent ambitions. The Queen learned that a wife who is beaten by her husband may nonetheless profit from the pity she excites, that mothers-in-law and daughters-in-law rarely get on, that most marriages are less than happy, that large dogs are dangerous pets – and that migrating birds simply follow the coastline(!). She also learned that George IV did not grieve over the death of his daughter, that his mistress was rapacious and that his mother spoke with a thick accent. Melbourne made the Queen feel the one bright flower of a jaded stock.

It was as if her education had been in black and white and Melbourne was now supplying the colours. There can be no question that he enormously enriched her knowledge of the world and of the society over which she was going to preside. Melbourne was like a delightful finishing-school after a sober convent education, like taking a grand tour after reading a Baedeker, like a debutante party following a school picnic.

Politically, however, his educative value was far less valuable. In some ways it was actually unfortunate. Never has a greater opportunity been missed; never did a prime minister have his sovereign more completely at his disposal. In that first year of her reign the Queen was willing to learn almost any lesson from Melbourne. He did, to some extent, inculcate her with his political philosophy, but it was not a philosophy very useful to a nineteenth-century monarch. Melbourne seems never to have formulated articulately his own view of the constitutional role of the sovereign, but insofar as one can make it out, he believed that the Crown was possessed of very definite powers, which should always be at the disposal of the prime minister. The sovereign, so to speak, had to lend his power to the prime minister, and he had to lend it to each prime minister in turn, no matter how much the political views of the incumbent varied from those of his predecessor. This was a very different view from the one which was later to be espoused by Prince Albert and his political mentor, Baron Stockmar, which, very briefly, placed the Crown above political parties, giving it a role of impartial umpire. According to Melbourne, the Crown had to be first a violent

Whig and then a violent Tory. According to Albert, it should be neither.

Melbourne's doctrine was not the doctrine to teach the young Victoria. She was perfectly willing to accept the first part of his theory and to turn herself into a violent Whig, but she had no idea of changing her party sympathies when the government should change. Melbourne should have foreseen that a strong-minded and passionate young woman was not easily going to turn herself into the political chameleon that he visualized. He made Victoria's job harder, for she had to re-learn her role under Albert, and then again, after Albert, she had to make her own terms with a third and soon prevailing political theory that conceived of the sovereign as having virtually no powers at all.

Victoria's reign started like a brilliant spring after the long foggy winter of her lunatic grandfather and quixotic uncles. The sternest faces smiled at the image of a young fresh female face under the crown. In the first year the praises were universal. She had such charm, such grace, such an air about her; she seemed to care so about everyone and everything! Surely, a great era was dawning. But honeymoons cannot last forever. Within a year the scandalmongers had their teeth in a juicy plum: the Court's treatment of the unhappy Lady Flora Hastings.

She was a maid of honour to the Duchess of Kent, who had been with Victoria and her mother for some years prior to the accession but who had never been popular with the Queen. This hostility appears to have originated with rumours of Lady Flora's intimacy with the detested Conroy. It was even said that she and Sir John had made the journey from Scotland to London alone, in the same carriage. When Lehzen, therefore, observed that Lady Flora's waistline appeared to be expanding, although there had been no alteration in her unmarried state, the Queen followed her friend's glances with a sharp and critical eye. It did not take long for her to be convinced. 'We have no doubt that she is – to use plain words – with child!' she entered censoriously in her diary. 'The horrid cause of all this is the monster and demon incarnate, whose name I forebear to mention.'

The Queen confided her suspicions in Melbourne who was, of course, most anxious not to have the Crown embroiled in any scandal. He strongly urged silence. But he proved totally unable to control the disastrous development of the affair. The Queen's long smouldering hatred of her mother at last had a definite and vulnerable target. The situation was in part Melbourne's fault. He had fanned the flames of the family quarrel by discussing the Duchess of Kent in terms of the greatest candour. 'Talked of my dislike of Mama,' one royal entry runs. 'Lord M said that she was a liar and a hypocrite.' 'I never saw so foolish a woman,' Melbourne had told the Queen on another occasion. 'Which', she notes, 'is very true, and we both laughed!'

The pleasure that the Queen derived in making these entries goes far to show how passionate her resentment of her mother was. An ordinary filial hostility will receive a quick check when the child finds that it is shared by another person. If Victoria had not detested the Duchess in all sincerity, she would have frowned when her minister described her parent as a liar and a hypocrite. But Victoria evidently welcomed this confirmation of what she herself had long believed. Melbourne may have found that he was quite unable to govern her when she got her hands on evidence that she probably thought would destroy Conroy.

The unfortunate Lady Flora Hastings, maid of honour to the Duchess of Kent. Her illness and tragic death, after a Court scandal caused by baseless gossip, made Victoria unpopular.

It was bad enough that a physical examination proved that Lady Flora was not pregnant. It was worse when her brother demanded a public apology. Melbourne fumbled the whole business and aggravated the situation by his efforts to keep the Queen clear of all criticism. It would have been far better had he got her to make a public apology or at least offered one on her behalf. But he delayed and dallied and prevaricated until the Hastings family, exasperated and perhaps incited by Conroy, took the whole affair to the Press. What in the end precipitated the worst uproar of all was that poor Lady Flora, as if to have the last word even at the cost of her life, sickened and died. The swelling in her abdomen had been a malignant tumour. The horrified Queen, now genuinely repentant, heard herself greeted with cries of 'Mrs Melbourne' when she drove through the streets of London.

Nothing, however, seemed to shake the Queen's devotion to her first minister. Commenting in her journal on Melbourne's use of the clause 'so long as he held the confidence of the Crown', she wrote: 'God knows, no minister, no friend, ever possessed it so entirely as this truly excellent Lord Melbourne possesses mine!' Only three years after this entry, the now happily married diarist would note beside it: 'Reading this again I cannot forebear remarking what an artificial state of happiness mine was then, and what a blessing it is I have now, in my beloved husband, real and solid happiness which no politics … can change.'

Yet even when she testified, in 1839, to her absolute confidence in Melbourne, her attitude was changing. If she was still devoted, she was less submissive. If she still needed him, she was beginning to take in that he needed *her*. He was less the leader now, more part of her team. And if anyone should try to break up that team, he would find that the Queen was capable of acting quite independently to preserve it. Let him beware! The Hanovers, after all, had Tudor blood.

When Melbourne at last lost his majority in the House of Commons, and the Duke of Wellington advised the Queen to send for Sir Robert Peel and ask him to form a government, she acted as if a personal wrong had been done her. As Melbourne agreed with the Duke, she had no alternative, but she reached about desperately for a spike to stick in Sir Robert's wheel. She found one. When Sir Robert made the entirely fitting request that at least half her ladies should be wives of Tories, she refused to make a single alteration in her household. She was even passionately indignant that he should have presumed to ask this of her. Melbourne, first learning of this, thought that the Queen had, with perfect propriety, resisted a demand by Sir Robert that she replace *all* her ladies with Tories. When he discovered the true situation, he was appalled at what she had done. He began to realize that he had been dealing with a much stronger character than he had thought. Without going so far as to liken his situation to that of Frankenstein when his monster got out of control, one can imagine what grave misgivings he must have had when he received this strong missive from Buckingham Palace, dated 9 May 1839:

The Queen writes one line to prepare Lord Melbourne for what *may* happen in a very few hours. Sir Robert has behaved very ill, he insisted on my giving up my Ladies, to which I replied that I *never* would consent, and I never saw a man so frightened; he said he must go to the Duke of Wellington and consult with him, when both would return – and he said this must suspend all further proceedings, and he asked if I would be ready to receive a decision, which I said I would; he was quite perturbed. I said, besides many other things, that if he or the Duke of W. had been at the head of the Government when I came to the Throne, perhaps there might have been a *few* more Tory Ladies, but that then if you had come into office you would *never* have *dreamt* of changing them. I was calm but very decided, and I think you would have been pleased to see my composure and great firmness. Keep yourself in readiness, for you may soon be wanted.

To her journal the Queen related the scene between herself and Sir Robert with evident satisfaction at how effectively she had handled it. She gloried in her own intransigence and her refusal to offer the smallest compromise. Was not this how the great Elizabeth would have handled such impertinence?

Soon after this, Sir Robert said, 'Now about the Ladies,' – upon which I said I could *not* give up *any* of my Ladies, and never had imagined such a thing; he asked if I meant to retain *all*; *all*, I said; the Mistress of the Robes and the Ladies of the Bedchamber? he asked. I replied *all*; for he said they were the Wives of the Opponents of the Government; mentioning Lady Normanby in particular, as one of the late Ministers' wives. I said that would not interfere, I never talked Politics with them, and that they were related, many of them, to Tories; and I enumerated those of my Bedchamber Women and Maids of Honour; upon which he said he didn't mean *all* the Bedchamber Women and *all* the Maids of Honour, he meant the Mistresses of the Robes and the Ladies of the Bedchamber, – to which I replied *they* were of more consequence than the others, and I could *not* consent, and that it had never been done before; he said I was a Queen Regnant, and that made the difference; not here, I said, – and I maintained my right.

Melbourne was now called in to receive the Queen's account of just what had happened. As she describes this in her journal, she makes it appear that he entirely agreed with what she had done, but one is not at all sure that he was as satisfied as she assumes. He went along with her because she was the sovereign and because she had done it for him and also because it resulted in the continuation of his office, which he naturally desired. But when he speaks of the 'very serious consequences' that the Queen's action may have, one certainly does not get the impression that he thought things as rosy as she did.

I repeated many of my arguments, all of which pleased Lord M. and which he agreed to; amongst others – that I said to the Duke, was Sir Robert so weak that *even* the Ladies must be of his opinion? The Duke denied that. The Duke then took my decision to Sir Robert, who was waiting in the next room; after a few minutes Sir Robert returned – and I have already related what then took place. I also told Lord M. that I said to Sir Robert that as I had wished him to be frank, he would wish me to be so; and I therefore said that he must make allowance for my feelings, as I had been always brought up in very strong feelings on the other (Whig) side, and that my feelings had always been very strongly with my Government, therefore my feelings could not easily change, though I might be fair; and Lord M. approved all, and saw and said I could not do otherwise. I acted quite alone,

OVERLEAF Winterhalter's painting of Victoria and Albert with their five eldest children.

I said, and feared I might have embarrassed the Government. 'I must summon the Cabinet,' said Lord M., 'at once; it may have very serious consequences; if we can't go on with this House of Commons, we may have to dissolve Parliament, and we don't know if we may get as good a House of Commons.'

Sir Robert's refusal to form a government resulted in the continuation of Melbourne's ministry for another two years, which is certainly proof of the considerable power that the Crown still had in the middle of the nineteenth century. Melbourne knew perfectly well that things had now got slightly out of hand, and he belatedly dedicated his wisdom and tact to the job of restoring the Queen to a more proper constitutional balance. The first thing to persuade her to do was to moderate her strong Whig feelings and to prepare herself for the inevitable: a Tory ministry in the near future. From now on Melbourne began to intersperse in their conversations carefully-placed remarks, however seemingly casual, to the effect that Tories, after all, were not so bad; that, when all was said and done, there was not much to choose between any two political parties. This was certainly in Melbourne's natural vein, but the Queen pounced on each statement and indicated her clear dissent, which she would then record in her journal. Here is one entry in which she shows immediate alarm at the idea that the crisis of the ladies of the bedchamber might come again:

I said, as for the Tories, I never would apply to them; I must, in some shape, he said; I never would submit about the Ladies; that must be arranged, he said. But why speak of all this *now*? I said, there was no fear *now*? 'I don't know,' he said. I said, as the others (the Tories) admitted *themselves* they could not stand, they ought to help and not to oppose every reasonable measure, as they had done, and not behave as they had done in the House of Lords. 'They didn't behave so badly in the House of Lords,' said Lord M. (This is admirable fairness.) 'They didn't throw out many bills.' But altered a good many, I said. 'But I don't know that those alterations didn't do them good,' said Lord M. laughing.

When the Queen went so far as to express her desire not to ask any Tories to the palace, Melbourne had to protest. As usual, she records his every word on the subject:

I said, I wished to ask none of the Tories this year. 'If you do that,' said Lord M., 'you, as it were, cut them off.' I observed John Russell disliked them; Lord M. said, 'I think J. Russell has a good deal of bitter personal feeling,' which he didn't show, but which extended towards the Tories pretty generally. '*I* don't dislike the Tories,' said Lord M., 'I think they are very much like the others.' We agreed J. Russell disliked being supported by them. 'I don't care,' said Lord M., 'by whom I am supported; I consider them all as one; I don't care by whom I'm helped, as long as I *am* helped,' he said laughing.

The identification of the Queen with her Whig minister following the scandal of Lady Flora Hastings reduced the royal popularity to a point where the Queen was actually hissed at Ascot by two ladies, one of whom was the Duchess of Montrose. This made her so angry that she said they should be horsewhipped. Melbourne protested that she was taking the episode much too seriously:

'You shouldn't give way too much to personal dislikes,' said Lord M., and he alluded to the 2 ladies who everybody knows hissed when I came up the course. 'Now, are you sure they did it?' he asked; 'quite sure.' 'They did it at me,' he said; 'that was just the same,' I replied, and that I knew they did it at me also. 'I heard it,' he said, 'some of the women told me.' I said I had every reason to be very angry with Peel. 'You both say just the same,' said Lord M., 'he says, "I feel I can never be the Queen's Minister," and you say he never can be your Minister.' I said that was so. 'It's very odd that two such interviews should have produced so much irritation,' said Lord M.

Fortunately for the British constitutional process, when Melbourne's tottering government fell at last, and Sir Robert Peel became prime minister, the Queen was married to Albert and too entranced with her bridegroom to raise much further fuss over her ladies of the bedchamber. What she would not learn from Melbourne she would learn, as we shall see, from her husband and Stockmar. They indoctrinated her with constitutional principles but not, alas, always the ones that were going to prevail. So long as Albert lived, Victoria had the benefit of his great good sense in knowing when not to push too far his ideas of constitutional monarchy. But when he was gone, the Queen was left alone with a rather anachronistic philosophy of where her duties lay. She got through; she always got through. That is something one can never quite get away from: that in her own indefinable way Victoria always managed to end up on top of her problem. Perhaps it was simply that she was a great queen. But Melbourne had not made her job any easier.

Chapter Two

ALBERT THE GOOD

Prince Leopold of Coburg with his wife, Princess Charlotte of Wales, whose tragic death in childbirth placed Victoria second in line to the English throne.

A principal industry of the German States in the nineteenth century was the production of marriageable princes and princesses. The reigning families of Europe had, by and large, to marry among each other. It was not fitting for the heir to a crown to marry a subject, and it was even less desirable for him to marry somebody else's. To avoid this problem, he had to confine his search to royalties, and no part of Europe had a vaster quantity of these than the thirty-eight states into which the German confederation had been divided by the Treaty of Vienna in 1815. Each state had a reigning family, and though many were penniless, all had the necessary 'royal' or 'serene' highness before their names, and they were more or less evenly divided between Protestants and Catholics. Beauty of person, when it appeared in a candidate, was a trump card. After all, there was no particular political value in marrying a Hesse-Darmstadt or a Saxe-Meiningen, and there was certainly no dower to be anticipated. So if a princess of one little royal house was more enticing than that of another, the choice was easily made. Thus, Princess Alexandra of Schleswig-Holstein-Sonderburg-Glucksburg, without a penny to her name and with a political affiliation which was bound to make any prince who chose her obnoxious to Prussia, was nonetheless able to prefer the Prince of Wales to the Czarevitch, while a generation later Alexandra of Hesse, equally beautiful and no better dowered, was able to turn down the Duke of Clarence, heir to the British throne, to marry the future Czar Nicholas II.

The House of Coburg in Saxony, although a very old and distinguished one, did not make its first great international alliance until its Princess Juliana married the Grand Duke Constantine of Russia in 1796, a match which helped to pave the way for the even better one of her younger sister to a son of George III of England. Juliana's marriage was not happy, but it brought her brother Leopold a commission in the Russian army and to the notice of some very important persons in the brilliant military assembly which occupied Paris in 1815. Leopold, who had great

PREVIOUS PAGE Prince Albert of Saxe-Coburg-Gotha by Winterhalter.

38

ambition, sharp brains and, most importantly, dazzling good looks, made the greatest match of any Coburg to that date, the greatest match, indeed, in all Europe, to the Princess Charlotte of Wales, heiress presumptive of the Prince Regent, later George IV. Her death in childbirth before that of her father seemed to check the Coburg advance, but the check was only temporary. Leopold still had his looks and an English pension of £50,000 per annum, and his wife's death, if it deprived him of the British crown, ensured it to his own niece, the Princess Victoria of Kent.

Leopold's grief, however, was not feigned. He loved Charlotte, and his deep despondency might have impeded his ambition had he not been prompted by a shrewd and sagacious aide who saw

An engraving of Baron Stockmar, Leopold's private secretary and mentor to Prince Albert.

in the House of Coburg a God-sent tool for nothing less than the spiritual regeneration of Europe. Baron Stockmar, an army doctor, had met Leopold in the wars and joined his staff. They soon became intimate, and when Leopold went to England, Stockmar accompanied him as his private secretary, not as his doctor. Indeed, he declined to treat the Princess Charlotte in her last illness, preferring to have her butchered by an incompetent English medical man to having her possible death under his care blamed on a foreigner. Yet she had become devoted to her husband's funny little aide and died crying 'Stocky, Stocky'. The least he could do for the poor creature was to look after her widower.

What was available? Greece. Negotiations were entered into for the empty throne, but it proved too precarious. The new state of Belgium looked more promising. Stockmar helped to arrange the deal. A Coburg became King Leopold I and a son-in-law of the French King, Louis Philippe. The British pension had to be given up, but not before a modest but adequate allowance for life had been carved out of it for the faithful aide.

Independent now, even of Leopold, Stockmar looked about to see what next he could do with the handsome princes of Coburg. Princess Victoria was obviously the great prize. She was herself a Coburg, of course, but only on the distaff side, and her mother was a goose. Leopold and Stockmar, looking forward to a new age of royalty, when Europe was to be governed by constitutional monarchs of high moral character, perceived that Victoria, whose position would be the greatest of all, must be rescued from the dissolute traditions of her Hanoverian antecedents by a noble prince of their own choosing. Their candidate was Albert, second son of Leopold's oldest brother, the reigning duke of Saxe-Coburg-Gotha.

The English royal family was hostile to the Coburgs, but its members were ageing, disunited and frivolous. The keystone of the Leopold–Stockmar plan was Victoria's mother, the Duchess of Kent, who had absolute control of her child and who might be presumed, as regent for an infant queen, to have the final voice in her matrimonial plans. Victoria and Albert were young; Victoria's reigning uncle, William IV, was old. There was time, and it was on Stockmar's side. He kept his hand in by journeying to Lisbon to arrange the marriage of yet another Coburg prince, Ferdinand, son of Leopold's brother of that name, to the widowed Maria II, queen regnant of Portugal.

The big job was now the training of Albert for his future role.

OPPOSITE ABOVE A portrait of William Lamb, 2nd Viscount Melbourne, by J. Partridge, executed in 1844.

OPPOSITE BELOW Prince Albert by Winterhalter, painted in 1842.

OVERLEAF 'The Inauguration by Her most gracious majesty Queen Victoria and his royal highness the Prince Albert of the Exhibition of the Industry of all Nations, May the 1st 1831,' by David Roberts.

He was a gentle, charming lad with a passion for natural history, who loved to roam and hunt in the Thuringian forests and who showed no interest at all in the world of Courts and power. Yet he seemed, as a conscientious and unquestioning junior, to have accepted docilely his doom. His uncle and the Baron had the wisdom to present it to him entirely as a duty, never as a pleasure. Of course, Victoria might refuse him, but the training would not be lost. Another queen regnant might turn up. And if not . . . well, what else could one *do* with German princelings? Albert was sent to Bonn for a comprehensive education in languages, philosophy and science, and then to Italy, with Stockmar, to learn about ladies and drawing-rooms. The latter course he never passed, but, as in everything else, he made sincere efforts.

There had been little feminine atmosphere in the boy's upbringing. His parents had been divorced, a most rare occurrence in reigning families, and his mother, whom he had hardly known, had died young in Paris, where she had moved with her second husband. Rumours of her infidelities, even of Albert's possible bastardy, are probably without basis. It is notable that he and Victoria gave her name, Louise, to their fourth daughter. But the lack of a mother's love must have had an impact. Perhaps it was that which made her sons what they became: Ernest, a rake; Albert, a prig. Certainly, it was Albert and not Victoria who brought prudishness to the British Court. He had a horror of all sexual intercourse outside marriage which was almost physical in its violence. Perhaps he equated it with the venereal disease that early afflicted his brother. He was later to insist that everyone in the royal circle be beyond reproach, even objecting to the appointment of Cabinet ministers of doubtful reputation. If Victoria adopted his standards in later life, it was out of reverence for his memory. She had started with a healthier attitude.

A hitch in the Baron's plans was occasioned by the longevity of William IV, who did not expire until his heiress-presumptive had attained her majority at the age of eighteen. Instead of the compliant infant child of a Coburg regent, Stockmar had now to cope with a spirited young woman, of a decided independence of mind, who found herself suddenly at the helm of the most powerful empire in the world. The very first thing that she did was to separate herself from her mother. It was fortunate, to say the least, that Stockmar had not allowed Leopold to become too closely identified with the Duchess of Kent. Victoria's deep affection for her uncle was the cornerstone on which Stockmar had

William IV, whose longevity caused a delay in Baron Stockmar's ambitious plans for the marriage of Albert to Victoria.

OPPOSITE 'Queen Victoria, the Prince of Wales and the Princess Royal' by Sir Francis Grant.

to build his project, when he came over to England, one of the earliest visitors to the new Court.

He found the Queen very clear and definite in her attitudes. She adored her possessive but idolizing governess, the Baroness Lehzen, who had taken her mother's place, and her Prime Minister, Lord Melbourne, the charming and cynical old Whig aristocrat who made affairs of state so amusing for her, even if he laughed at too many things. She disliked her stupid, pig-headed mother and detested the latter's unscrupulous steward and possible lover, Sir John Conroy. She loved balls and palaces and handsome, dashing young men. She delighted in the whole adventure of being the young sovereign of a great and growing empire. She had a generous heart.

Her preparation for the job, as Stockmar well knew, had been far from ideal. She had grown up, an only child (her half-brother and half-sister on her mother's side had been too much older to be companions), without a father, without friends or even companions her own age, in the constant company of a dominating mother who hoped to achieve authority through her. The Duchess, in turn, had been dominated by the wicked Conroy, who had done everything in his power, short of physical force, to gain an ascendancy over the young Princess. Victoria must have lived in a strange limbo, knowing that a great world existed beyond her confined one, and a great future beyond her small present. But if her isolation kept too many things away from her, it may also have helped to preserve some that were fine within herself.

She had emerged from this cocoon a unique figure among royalties. She was absolutely honest and absolutely loyal. She was determined to be a good queen, and she never relaxed this determination. She had a clear, literal mind, a prodigious memory, and she did not shrink from work. She was strong and healthy, though short of stature, with a brief bloom of prettiness which soon succumbed to a sturdy, plain stoutness. On the debit side were a will that poured over into stubbornness, a hot temper and a bossiness which the Crown, needless to say, did nothing to diminish. What Stockmar divined was that under the bristling front was a passionate and very feminine woman. As yet she hardly knew Albert, having seen him only once, when he was a fat and easily tired sixteen-year-old. But she knew all about her uncle's plans and did not object, so long as she had her fun first. After all, she would have to marry some day.

Stockmar did not hurry her. She had first to get used to being queen. He reminded her gently of her uncle's devotion, of Leopold's help to her mother and herself in more difficult times, of his loans when George IV had been stingy. He flattered and placated Lehzen. He offered sound, practical advice. He never insisted, never overstayed his welcome. He seemed to have no personal axe to grind. He was a great convenience to a young, inexperienced sovereign, and Victoria had the sense to see this. It may be significant that the two bad mistakes of this brief unmarried portion of her reign (her harsh treatment of Lady Flora Hastings and her insistence on retaining the Whig Ladies of the Bedchamber after Melbourne's first fall) both occurred during absences of Stockmar on the Continent.

What card could Albert now play? Sex appeal. It was the only one. Stockmar knew all about it. It was his ace of trumps. At just the right moment, when the Queen was beginning, after two years, to be a bit disillusioned with the delights of rule, when she had experienced the chill of her first bout with adverse public opinion and was feeling the need of something from the men around her other than Melbourne's amused, cynical, paternal affection and his turning of everything into jokes, Albert was produced. He was ripe with the briefness of a ripe melon. Three years earlier, on his only previous visit to England, he had been in his awkward teens; a few years later he would already be showing symptoms of premature middle age: baldness and a pot. But in that October of 1839 he was perfect. Victoria wrote at once to Uncle Leopold: 'Albert's *beauty* is *most striking*, and he so amiable and unaffected – in short very *fascinating*.' Three days later she wrote to announce their engagement. In four months they were married.

It is doubtful if Victoria could have known her twenty-year-old husband very well. What she saw was the dream prince from the northern forests, grave, gentle and serene. She had him painted by Robert Thorburn, in armour. 'Most beautiful indeed,' the portrait was, according to Lady Lyttleton, 'quite his gravest, manliest look, and done when he was rather tanned.' But there was another side to the Prince, a stiff, Teutonic side. He rarely deviated from the strictest etiquette, sitting through long operas while ladies-in-waiting stood behind his chair. There was even a touch of cruelty in his character, manifested in the rather terrible things that he would later have to say in the long, cool, reasoned memoranda that he sent to his wife when she lost her

One of Albert's favourite occupations was shooting, and stag hunting in Scotland probably reminded him of the *battues* of his native Coburg. This painting by Landseer depicts the Prince presenting his stag to the Queen by Loch Muich.

OPPOSITE The painting of Prince Albert in armour by Robert Thorburn which Victoria commissioned.

temper. And then there were the *battues*.

In 1845, when he took his bride on her first visit to Coburg, they were guests at this brutal sport. Sir Theodore Martin has described it. A space was cleared in the heart of the forest and closed in with canvas hangings. In the centre, covered with branches and firs and decorated with wreaths of flowers, was a pavilion destined to receive the distinguished visitors. When they had entered it, part of the canvas was let down and a number of stags and hinds dashed into the enclosure. The firing began from the pavilion, and fifty-five head of game, thirty-one of them stags, were seen stretched upon the ground, while the music of a band played. Sir Theodore relates that, after this butchery, 'it was pleasant to turn from it once more to the beautiful woodland vistas and the emerald meadows high in the heart of the forest'. One imagines that it was.

In the first two years of marriage, however, the sylvan prince, grave, reflective, at times a bit moody, was still predominant. Albert, indeed, seemed almost too passive under the series of initial humiliations to which he was subjected. He was given no title, no proper precedence, and Parliament allotted him only sixty per cent of Uncle Leopold's figure of £50,000. He could not even choose his own private secretary: he had to make do with a former secretary of Melbourne's. He protested, then gave way. He appeared to be resigned to play the role of companion for the sovereign's leisure hours, a lover to be summoned when wanted, a charming German toy to be kept out of the 'real world' of politics and Cabinet officers. His situation was worse than that of a queen consort, for he was not even allowed to interfere in the management of the royal household. There chaos, corruption and the inefficient but officious Lehzen ruled. And was there not something ridiculous about a salaried German import, kept for breeding purposes? Albert, aimlessly reading or wandering in the Windsor woods with his gun, might have been a melancholy Hamlet without even the dignifying motivation of revenge.

Victoria could not have been an easy wife. She was too deeply self-absorbed. The quality of relating everything immediately to her own strong initial reaction may have made her a great journalist, but it did not make her a great spouse. Her poor fiancé must have felt sadly put down when he received the following reminder from his bride-to-be: 'You forget, my dearest love, that I am the sovereign, and that business can stop and wait for nothing ... as an English prince you have no right ... to quarter the English arms, but the Sovereign has the power to allow it by Royal Command; this was done for Uncle Leopold by the Prince Regent, and I will do it again for you. But it can only be done by Royal Command.'

She loved Albert passionately and wanted him to be happy, but he was to be happy in the role that she selected. It is easy to blame her for this, but if one considers her appalling upbringing and the difficulties of adjustment to her exalted position, it is astonishing that she was not more selfish than she was. Imagine the shock of being translated, overnight, from a child who had to share her bedroom with 'Mama' and submit her diary to be read, to a mighty monarch with a charming old wizard of a premier to take her by the hand and show her all the glories of the world! That she should *never*, after such a heady start, have deviated from her own rigid sense of duty is much more extraordinary than that she should have exaggerated the duty of others to herself.

The biographers are divided as to what Albert felt towards Victoria. Lytton Strachey was of the opinion that Albert was never in love with her; more recent scholars think that he was. But what does 'in love' mean? My own impression is that he clearly cared less for her than she for him, but then I doubt that he had the passion in his nature that she had. I suggest that he was a highly domestic animal, devotedly attached to his small spouse and large family. Perhaps he was as much in love as he was capable of being. It seems to have been generally conceded that he never, before or after marriage, showed the smallest sexual interest in any other woman. Nor is there the slightest evidence, outside the usual gossip attaching to all royalties, of any deviant inclinations.

Were the Queen's sexual demands too great for him? Obviously, she had a sharp need for every aspect of marital devotion, which may explain her near insanity on Albert's death. I find it easy to imagine that she may have wanted to make love more frequently than he did, but there is nothing to suggest that he was not usually ready and willing to comply. The Queen was probably fairly easily satisfied; she had no one to compare him with, nobody even to discuss such matters with. Sex must have been an easy price for the peace and quiet that he craved. It may, too, have warded off the temper tantrums that he so dreaded. There is some reason to suspect that he shared Stockmar's fear that frustration might bring out in Victoria a latent family insanity. It was better to make love than to face another George III.

But outside the bedroom Albert showed, at first, little ability in handling her. When the Queen exploded during arguments and even threw things at him, he would retire to his study to make out a long list of all the reasons that he was right and she was wrong. It was his way of managing everything to pour out his mind on paper, to interpose between himself and an irrational universe the crowded pages of his irrefutable logic. How else could these uncouth islanders and their violent queen be handled? How often, in those first two years, with Lord Melbourne in charge of Victoria the queen, and Lehzen in charge of Victoria the housewife, must he have yearned for the deep green and blessed stillness of Thuringian forests!

Help, however, was on the way. Stockmar had observed all that was going on. The only real danger to his plans was Albert's lassitude and lack of interest in politics. Stockmar now dedicated all his time to the problems of the royal couple. He forced Albert to face the responsibilities of his role as consort. He pointed out to him over and over again that the situation was precarious. Victoria did not really understand official business, and she had allowed herself, under Melbourne's spell, to become the tool of the Whigs. The Crown was in danger as a result of such political partisanship, and it was clearly Albert's duty to take the lead, both in politics and in his own home. Victoria, deep down, was yearning for a strong husband. She did not *want* to make all the

Baroness Lehzen who, as
a result of an ultimatum
issued to Victoria by
Albert, quietly retired to
a cottage in Hanover.
Painting after a miniature
at Windsor Castle.

decisions. If Albert desired proof of his own strength, let him start
with Lehzen. Let him get rid of the odious Baroness. After that,
he would see that the world was his!

A stronger man might not have treated the poor old governess
as Albert did. He would have relegated her to a wing of the castle
and allowed her to cluck over the royal children at carefully speci-
fied hours. And had Albert been able to foresee the completeness
of his own victory, he might have been more moderate. But he
did not foresee it. He saw himself as the helpless victim of a hostile
Parliament, the laughing-stock of a cruel public, the chattel of
a wife who was treating him as a puppet. Could his enemies not
strike at him with impunity? Was he even safe? In his panic he
sometimes imagined that Lehzen was actually trying to kill him.
Why had he not been warned about a viciously bucking horse,
or ice at Windsor too thin for skating? He was fighting for his
very life, and who but a fool would give quarter in such a
struggle?

At last he decided that the time had come for the great test.
He presented Victoria with what was virtually an ultimatum: if
she wanted a loving husband and a happy home, Lehzen must
go. The Queen and Albert departed for a visit, and Lehzen for
once was left behind. Stockmar now seized the opportunity to
warn her of the ultimate hopelessness of fighting a husband and
father. How could a mere governess win against such odds? He
probably hinted that her pension might be in danger. Lehzen was
no fool; she saw the handwriting all over the wall. Quietly, she
retired to a cottage in Hanover. I own the copy of General Grey's
volume on the younger years of the Prince Consort which Queen
Victoria sent to Lehzen some years after Albert's death. It is inscribed 'to dearest Lehzen, in recollection of former happy days'.
Lehzen must have had rather different recollections of those days,
but at least she could reflect that she had survived her old
opponent.

Like most royal favourites, Lehzen had craved the show of
power. She loved her position in the palace and the fawning respect that was shown to her. It was all that she did crave, but
it was enough. Stockmar had a different kind of egotism, if indeed
he had any at all. He liked to remain behind the scenes, unrecog-
nized, except by a handful of the greatest in the land. He would
arrive from Coburg without suite or fanfare, a simple German
gentleman, and would put up quietly in a spare room in Buckingham Palace or at Windsor, consulting privately with the

Queen and the Prince until such time as he saw fit to disappear again on a mission or to his native land. As he said in his memoirs: 'Like a thief in the night, I have often laid the seedcorn in the earth, and when the plant grew up and could be seen I knew how to ascribe the merit to others.' Of course, it is possible that such modesty was merely the cover of a deeper and fiercer pride. It might have been his ecstasy, and a sufficient reward for all his labours, simply to behold the change of expression on the face of some grand butler, who had been inclined perhaps to deny admission to this drab little foreigner, when he beheld his master, a Sir Robert Peel or a Lord Melbourne, hurrying from the drawing-room into the hall with outstretched arms exclaiming 'My dear Baron, what an honour to have you here!' On the other hand, Stockmar may have have been genuinely selfless, a man with a mission, perfectly content if that mission were simply accomplished.

The exile of Lehzen marks the beginning of Albert's rule. It is time to take a considered view of him. Here is how Mary Ponsonby, one of the Queen's ladies and the wife of her private secretary, summed him up:

That he was a happy man I very much doubt, for with all his love of dry formulas there was a strong vein of poetical feeling unexpressed even to himself. But it showed itself in his appreciation of music and his feeling of keen pain at the miseries of other lives, all of which one imagined to be discernible in the expression of his face, which at its best was sad and thoughtful. His manner was the least pleasing thing about him unless he was perfectly at his ease, and this rarely happened. There was a complete absence of that frankness which was such a charm in the Queen's manner, and there was also a self-consciousness which completely prevented one's recognition of being in the presence of a 'Grand Seigneur'. He gave one much more the idea of being an excellent tutor, and this was the cause of his being unpopular with those who judged entirely by his manner ... Looking carefully back and remembering his judgment on many points, I should say he was in ability on the level with a very intellectual German on the second line. He was without a spark of spontaneity, and this often made him put the commonest everyday occurrence into an abstract form, stating it as a proposition and treating it logically; whereas by the rapid application of common sense, lookers-on would arrive far nearer the truth in half the time ... The qualities of the Prince's character would place him, I think, on a far higher level than those of his mind. Unselfish, patient, kindhearted, truthful and just, one felt it was possible to rely upon him as upon a strong rock.

But a sense of humour? Mary Ponsonby could never discover it, unless it were to be found in the immoderate fits of laughter that seized the Prince at anything like a practical joke. Lord Granville used to say that it was idle to waste one's wit on the Queen and Prince when pretending to pinch one's finger in the door would send them into gales. The clumsy hunter who hid in the brush to shoot at stags and only wound them was the same man who roared if a courtier tripped over a mat or almost fell in the fire.

Stockmar was very proud of what he conceived to be his comprehension of the British Constitution. Under his interpretation, the balance of power between the three estates of Crown, Lords and Commons depended on the Lords as the centre of gravity. He believed that the Reform Bill of 1832 had moved this centre from the upper to the lower house, thereby throwing all political life into a 'state of feverish excitement and oscillation'. Only the 'moral purity of the Queen' could now safeguard the nation from the 'wild power of democracy'. It behoved the sovereign, guided by a spouse indoctrinated by Stockmar, to reassert her proper position as a permanent premier, ranking above the temporary head of the Cabinet and exercising supreme authority in all matters of discipline. Not only had the Queen power to dismiss every member of the Cabinet, according to the Baron; she need not even give her reasons! Such was the Constitution that Stockmar loved and honoured as 'the foundation, corner- and cope-stone of all the political civilization of the human race, present and to come'.

Albert swallowed it whole. Why not? To one born royal, it was a noble conception. The Crown was the supreme moral and political authority. Duty and power were agreeably mixed. Of course, Albert was not a king, but Stockmar had set the example of quashing ego. The Prince must learn to merge himself, lose himself, in the chief of state, but what was that but a way of becoming the chief of state? If a Christian lost his individuality in God, did he not become God, a part of God? 'The exaltation of royalty,' Albert wrote 'is possible only through the personal character of the sovereign.' The romantic prince whom Victoria had had painted as a knight in armour, the pure, idealistic leader, a Siegfried merged in King Arthur, would lead the British, and then perhaps the Germans, to a constitutional Europe, even a

Albert was a devoted father, and this lithograph from 1848 shows Victoria and Albert with the royal children and the Duchess of Kent round the Christmas table which became a yearly ritual.

constitutional world, where science and art would merge for the perfection of man. It would be toil; there would be no rest; but what did that matter with a goal so bright?

Once established as the Queen's private secretary, Albert was soon acting for her in everything. As Stockmar had rightly divined, she was really delighted to have somebody trustworthy to take the load off her back, and Albert was a glutton for work. As he himself was to describe his new functions, he was 'the natural head of her family, superintendent of her household, manager of her private affairs, sole confidential adviser in politics and only assistant in her communications with the officers of the Government'. When Napoleon III and Eugénie made their state visit during the Crimean War, it was Albert who sat in council with the Emperor and the generals, while Victoria, like a queen consort, chatted in the boudoir with Eugénie.

The political area that Albert chose for his very own was foreign affairs. Fluent in French, German and Italian and related to so many rulers, it was natural that he should consider himself more expert in the tangled web of European politics than the rather insular British statesmen of the epoch. But here it was his misfortune to run into headlong collision with Lord Palmerston, the Foreign Secretary, a man old enough to have been his father but quite unwilling to adopt the paternal role which Melbourne had found so pleasurable.

Palmerston was a difficult man for Albert to understand, being innately English in his contradictions. He worked for the abolition of slavery and favoured the Confederates. He championed the causes of revolution in Italy and Austria and supported flogging in the British army. He was a liberal who loved aristocratic society, a bellicose diplomat who knew when to make peace, a demon for work who delighted in the pleasures of the great country houses, a bully who could weep if occasion demanded it. Henry Adams has described his laugh: 'Ha! ... Ha! ... Ha!', slow, mechanical, wooden, 'a laugh of 1810 and the Congress of Vienna'. And unlike Albert, he was sceptical of ideals, eschewing great general policies and political objectives, contenting himself with preserving the status quo. If he had a policy, it was simply to prevent any power from becoming so strong as to threaten Britain.

It was intolerable for such a man to have to submit his dispatches to a snotty young German prince, imported purely for stud purposes, and to have them returned, after considerable

Lord Palmerston, the foreign secretary, clashed with both Victoria and Albert, and was nicknamed 'Pilgerstein' by the latter.

delay, with substantial corrections! Palmerston proceeded to by-pass the sovereign. When Victoria protested to Lord John Russell, the Prime Minister, Palmerston was told to correct his ways, but the by-passing continued. Victoria and Albert became vituperative in their rage. Albert, writing to Uncle Leopold, referred to Palmerston as 'Pilgerstein' and called him a 'heartless, obstinate and revengeful man'. But there was little that he or Victoria could do until Palmerston was caught in flat disobedience of Lord John himself, and then he was dismissed at the instigation of the Crown but not by the Crown. Yet the word got about that the famous old patriot had been dismissed at the request of the German consort, and Albert became dangerously unpopular.

The policy difference between the Crown (as represented by Albert) and Palmerston lay principally in the latter's inclination, when Britain's interests were not directly involved on the other side, to support the advance of democracy by popular movements in France, Italy and Portugal. Albert distrusted such movements in France because of his dislike of the French people, in Italy because of his Germanic sympathies with the Austrian overlords of Venetia and Lombardy, and in Portugal for the simple reason that the King-Consort was a Coburg. He was convinced that the Crown was entitled to a foreign minister subservient to the royal wish, and he never saw his own strong German bias as a disqualification for directing policy. On the contrary, he boasted that he would be a Coburg all his life.

Viewed from the point of view of his own era, his assumptions seem less arrogant. Royalty was more important then, and an argument could be made for viewing the contemporary German States as a force for international peace and order. Very few in Albert's day saw the imperial future of a militant Prussia which seemed instead to belong to Napoleon III. Nor was it entirely out of line for Albert to claim wider powers under the British Constitution for the Crown. His wife's uncles and grandfather had made stronger claims. Why should the House of Commons, a handful of rich men elected by a tiny fraction of the male population, and the House of Lords, elected by nobody, have been outraged by the idea that a sovereign might represent the people as well as, or even better than, themselves?

The answer is simple. Because they had the power, and Albert hadn't. Had he been born British and king in his own right, there is no telling what he might have accomplished. But he was a foreigner and a consort, and he was never allowed to forget it. During the Crimean War he was accused in the press of being pro-Russian, and there were crowds in London who actually gathered to see him taken to the Tower. But perhaps his bitterest moment came in 1855, at the low point of the Crimean War, when his wife was obliged to summon 'Pilgerstein' to the palace and to ask the grizzled old chauvinist, in a scene which forecast her great-grandson's bid to Churchill in 1940, to form a government. The 'moral purity' of the sovereign did not save her from having as her premier a man whose unauthorized entry into the bedchamber of one of her ladies-in-waiting had been discovered by the latter's screams!

Such, Albert learned, as the years dragged by, was the dreary way of the world, at least of a British world. He toiled on, but nothing ever came out quite as he intended. Life was certainly not malleable. He poured forth his advice on every conceivable subject in thousands, millions of words, on sanitation, duelling, public

housing and recreation, farming, armaments, morals, Italian unification, the Schleswig–Holstein question. Was there any gratitude, or even intelligent reaction, behind the endless pomposity
of the official acknowledgements: 'The Cabinet is deeply grateful
to His Royal Highness for his views on . . .'; 'The Prime Minister
was much impressed by what the Prince Consort had to state
about . . .'?

Perhaps he tried to drown his doubts in work. Sir Theodore
Martin describes the week beginning 14 October 1852:

The next day he distributes the prizes of the Windsor Royal Associa-
tion. On the 16th he meets Lord Derby, Lord Hardinge, Lord John
Manners, the Duke of Norfolk, the Dean of St Paul's, the Garter King
at Arms, and the Secretary of the Office of Works, to settle the complicated arrangements for the funeral of the Duke of Wellington. On
the 19th he is busy with negotiations for the purchase by the Exhibition
Commissioners of land at Kensington. Next day finds him engaged
with Mr Edgar Bowring in making the final corrections in the Report
of the Committee of the Commissioners, as to the disposal of the
Exhibition Surplus, a very elaborate and masterly document. The
same day he has to master the general results of the Cambridge
University Commission's Report, and to communicate them in his
capacity of Chancellor to the authorities of the University. On the
22nd he settles with Mr Henry Cole and Mr Redgrave the design of
the Duke of Wellington's funeral car. Two days afterwards, in a personal interview with Lord Derby, he goes into the details of the
Government measures, which are to consist of an acknowledgement
of Free Trade, Lightening of the burdens of Manufacture and Agri-
culture, Reduction of the Malt Tax, of the Duty on Tea, &c. On the
29th he presides at a meeting of the Exhibition Commissioners, at
which he persuades them to adopt his plan for the disposal of the surplus, and to vote further funds for the land purchases. The same day
he investigates the results of experiments made with Shrapnels at
Woolwich upon his recommendation, and writes an elaborate paper
to Lord Raglan on the subject. Again, a day or two afterwards, he
discusses the South Kensington project with the Chancellor of the
Exchequer, and goes fully into the financial details of the question
of National Defences; and then, passing from finance to art, settles
with Sir Archibald Macdonald the music to be played at the Duke
of Wellington's funeral.

Albert's compulsion to work grew until the days and nights were
not long enough for his toil. Ultimately, it undermined his health
and left him depressed and exhausted, an easy prey to the typhoid
fever that killed him. It affected his relationship with his wife,

who resented the diminishing amounts of time that he spent with her. It affected his relationship with his children, particularly the eldest son, because their rearing and education became part of his work load. It affected his relationship with the public, who wanted more showmanship and less greasy grind. He seemed to them a man who was determined to turn everything into a duty.

If only people would heed him! He was an early-nineteenth-century romantic who, like so many, had invested his idealism

The Queen's bedroom at Osborne House, built by Prince Albert out of the Queen's own funds. Victoria spent much of her leisure time at Osborne in later life.

in a passionate faith in science. There was nothing, no problems, large or small, that should not yield its secret to the patient and laborious analyst. As the years passed, Albert lost all sense of proportion. Nobody should be allowed to do anything but he, because he and only he could do it right. He selected Victoria's dresses; he designed her jewellery; he supervised every minute of his poor son Bertie's grim work-schedule; he pushed for a bigger navy; he tried to unite Germany!

I suggest that this compulsion and its attendant officiousness may explain the wide difference between the image of Albert to his contemporaries and his image to us. To many of the Queen's Cabinet he must have seemed not only an insufferable bore but a troublesome meddler. But to scholars today, who encounter in the Royal Archives his multitudinous memoranda, clearly conceived and cogently expressed, he seems like a statesman of vision. What we will never know is how many of them were even read.

If we take a survey of Albert's almost unlimited activities, we may conclude that he was most successful in the areas appropriate to the activities of a constitutional monarch or figurehead. He and Stockmar would have deeply resented this, but I believe it is true.

Take in the first place the reorganization of the royal household. Before Albert undertook this job, the Queen, like Louis XVI at Versailles, was a virtual prisoner in her own home, tied up and gagged in red tape. She could not have her windows cleaned, or even a fire lit, unless the appropriate servants co-operated. Guests at Windsor wandered vainly through the corridors in search of their rooms; luggage was lost; bells went unanswered. Victoria took it all for granted; she had been brought up that way. Lehzen, well served herself, gave the posts away to incompetent favourites. What the whole sorry mess needed was a Prussian drill-master, and that was what in effect it got. Albert's strictness, his orderliness, his capacity to organize, were here seen at their best. He swept out the Augean stables and rearranged the royal household so that it functioned with the efficiency and splendour that it manifests to this day. And he saved money, too, so much that he was able to build Osborne House and Balmoral Castle at the expense of the Crown!

In dealing summarily with the petty grafters of the royal pantry, Albert had no opposition of any significance. One can imagine Lord Palmerston's sigh of relief at the news that the meddlesome consort was so usefully engaged. But in Albert's greatest accomplishment, the great Crystal Palace exhibition, he had to face a certain amount of carping and heel-dragging, yet there was never any question that he had a perfect right to be doing what he was doing. Organizing an international exhibition of contemporary arts and industries in order to attract the leaders of the political and business worlds to London was precisely the kind of enterprise which needed a royal person as chairman, and as anyone knows who has ever been engaged in this kind of work, an honorary or 'do-nothing' chairman is *not* what is wanted. Every foot-pound of Albert's great energy and industry was needed and used before the Crystal Palace was finished and

The Great Exhibition of 1851, organized by Albert, was housed in an enormous canopy of steel and glass – the Crystal Palace. The trusses for the central aisle were raised with the help of cart-horses in the January of that year.

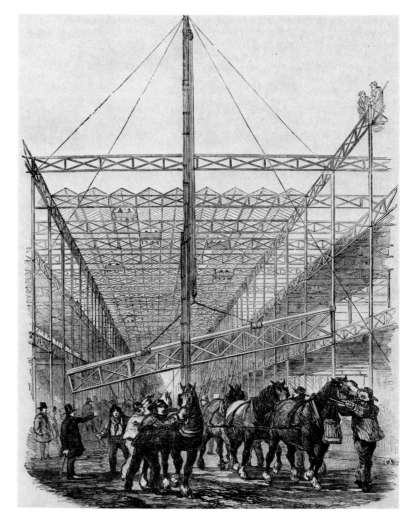

opened. It was a triumph, the one undoubted one of his career.

Turning now to a field less obviously the territory of a monarch, i.e. the training of the heir to the throne, we find Albert a total failure. It might seem that nothing could be more innately a father's duty than the education of his son, but with royal families this is not so. The whole nation had an interest in the education of the future Edward VII, but the nation was most certainly not consulted. What, after all, was more the favourite role of Stockmar than the rearing of princes? What was more fundamental to the Coburg philosophy of the divine right of constitutional monarchs? Albert and his old tutor drew up a formidable programme for the wretched lad.

There is a photograph which shows him and Stockmar and the royal tutors with Bertie. It demonstrates all too clearly why the system did not work. The poor Prince of Wales, awkward, at the gangling age, looks crushed and desperate. No wonder he struggled and raved! A great deal of nonsense has been written to excuse his father for this. It is perfectly true that he loved the boy, that he cared passionately for his well-being, and that he listened to critics of his plans. But one cannot get away from the fact that he was trying to make a human being into something which that human being was not, and that he was too stubborn and dogmatic to consider that he might be wrong. And when in the end he discovered that Bertie was actually having a love affair, his conduct was decidedly irrational. He went on as if the boy was lost forever. This attitude was considered just as odd in the British male world of 1861 as it would be today. Albert never made any sense in matters of sex.

And finally, when we move to a field which was clearly, at least by modern interpretation of the Constitution, beyond the province of the sovereign, foreign affairs, we find Albert again a failure, at least in the sense that he was unsuccessful in implementing his ideas. One can only conclude that his life would have been happier and more fruitful had he been blessed with an adviser more liberal and more English than Stockmar.

Stockmar had a dream even grander than the establishment of his own brand of constitutional monarchy in Britain: to establish it in Germany, a united Germany. What else would keep the demon of democracy at bay? Surely not the Latin nations. He and Albert both believed that freedom and justice were German

A portrait of Edward
in academic gown.

in their roots and that only disorder and ultimately despotism
could be expected from the more volatile races. Stockmar had
turned to Britain with its Constitution as the saviour of Europe,
but this was largely because Germany, separated into thirty-eight
states, had seemed incapable of the leadership that was required.
There had been the possibility of Prussia's taking a lead in German affairs, but Prussia had been obstinate and devoted to absolutism. Then there had been Austria, but Austria was too
occupied with her own multi-national problems and really not
quite sufficiently German for the job. But now, in the 1850s, it
began to seem possible again that Prussia might awaken, and

64

Stockmar focused his attention on the wonderful possibility of a German empire united under the command of a Hohenzollern.

He and Albert did not at first see eye to eye, because Albert, as a prince of Coburg, was unwilling to have the German mediatized rulers demoted as much as was necessary for the sake of unity, but Stockmar did not have much difficulty in persuading him. Might it not be possible for the German and British empires, in solid alliance, to lead the world to the blessings of constitutional government? Was it even necessary that it should be an alliance? Might these two great nations not be dynastically united? It was a heady dream, the headiest of all!

It seemed providential that Albert and Victoria's eldest daughter, Vicky, should have captured the heart of Fritz, son of the heir to the Prussian throne. She was young, only fifteen, and they had to wait two years, but in 1857 they were married, and it was a true love match. Vicky was as satisfactory to Albert as her brother Bertie was disappointing. If only she had been a boy! But then he would not have enjoyed the same intimacy with her. She was probably the only person whom Albert loved to the depth of his heart. She was bright and quick; she learned enthusiastically all he taught. She would take the torch that he had taken from Stockmar; she would bring liberalism and constitutional law to a Prussia which would one day be an empire. When she said farewell to her father, it was observed that they clung to each other and wept.

A photograph taken after the marriage of Vicky, the Princess Royal, to Prince Frederick (Fritz), oldest son of the heir to the Prussian throne. From left to right: Fritz, Prince Albert, Vicky, Prince Alfred, Prince Edward, Victoria, King Leopold.

A year later Vicky gave birth to a son. It is a common, even a rather vulgar, irony to point out that the first grandson of Stockmar's pupil, the infant destined to realize the dream, was the future Kaiser Wilhelm II. Of course, it is easy to make this out worse for poor Stockmar than it was. He and Albert never dreamed of the carnage of the First World War, much less the concentration camps of Adolf Hitler. They would have been appalled, undoubtedly. But the suspicion lingers that they would have been amenable to more German hegemony and authoritarianism than would have been palatable to most of Victoria's subjects. It is perfectly true that they both believed in constitutional restrictions, but the Hohenzollerns could still have made themselves sufficiently odious had they been subject merely to the checks of a Stockmar constitution. Gladstone once darkly quoted Albert as saying: 'We Germans have no boundaries.'

Long after Albert's death, the German son-in-law whose reign was tragically to be too short to implement the Stockmar ideal would describe it as follows:

I cannot help myself at this crisis from thinking a great deal of the plans my late father-in-law [the Prince Consort] as also the late King [Leopold I] of the Belgians, in conjunction with old Baron von Stockmar, entertained for a united Germany under a monarchical head. God so willed that those men should conceive the notion of a free German Imperial State, that in the true sense of the word should march at the forefront of civilization and be in a position to develop and bring to bear all noble ideals of the modern world, so that through German influence the rest of the world should be humanized, manners ennobled and people diverted from those frivolous French tendencies.

Perhaps one can visualize the two aspects of Albert's personality in his two most important grandsons: George V and the Kaiser. King George was sober, conscientious, industrious, a model constitutional monarch, Albert at his best. But he lacked Albert's brain-power. As one of his biographers privately remarked, his royal birth may have deprived the navy of a first-rate petty officer. The Kaiser, on the other hand, while lacking his cousin's fineness of character, had a much greater supply of imagination and ingenuity. He shared Stockmar's dream of a greater Germany, but his character was flawed by a quality not to be found in Stockmar or in his grandfather – that of an ass. The combination of George V and Wilhelm II on the throne in Berlin, an Albert who was a king and not just a consort, a German in Germany rather than a German in Britain, might in truth have saved Europe.

The birth of little Wilhelm in 1859, at any rate, seemed to mark the end of good things for Albert. Vicky had a horribly difficult childbirth, and the baby was left with a withered arm. What was almost worse was that Vicky was not proving popular in Berlin. Her in-laws did not seem at all disposed to find in her the qualities that the adoring father did. A German princess was not meant to be intellectual, political or brilliant. She was not meant to be her husband's partner but his slave. She was supposed to be docile, domestic, sweet; to be contented to gossip with other royal ladies and learn the German pedigrees. What kind of a creature was this bossy little Englishwoman? Was she her mother's agent? Was she a spy? When Stockmar went to Berlin to advise her, he did not find himself much more popular. One Prussian noble, asking a friend with whom he had been walking that morning and hearing that it was Stockmar, retorted: 'Why didn't you pitch him into the river?'

It was sad that Vicky should have been considered a 'Miss Fix-it', but for what other role had Albert prepared her? For what other role had he prepared himself? Did the world really want either of them? Had the British ever admired anything he had done so much as his riding to hounds? Albert brooded and fussed; his health deteriorated. On a visit to his beloved Coburg, during a walk in the woods, he was observed suddenly dissolved in tears.

Then the Duchess of Kent died. Thanks to Albert's intervention, relations between mother and daughter had been vastly improved. Albert had always liked his aunt and mother-in-law, and certainly, once she had accepted the loss of her influence, she had been a much more amenable creature. In her old age she became a placidly admiring mother, an adoring grandmother. But her death brought two new burdens to Albert at a time when he could least bear them. She had named him executor of her estate, which had many problems, and the Queen collapsed. Such a reaction to the death of a seventy-five-year-old parent whom, at least until her marriage, Victoria had frankly disliked, may seem undue, but there was probably much guilt in it. She pored through her mother's papers and wept afresh at each new bit of evidence of the latter's love for her. Poor Lehzen, in retrospect, instead of the friend who had stood between her and the machinations of Conroy, began to seem the agent, however innocent, of an evil destiny which had destroyed the most perfect of mother–daughter relationships. So violent was Victoria's grief

In 1861, the Duchess of Kent died, and Victoria exhibited a grief unusual for one who had positively disliked her mother, at least until the time of her marriage.

that people began to whisper that she was going the way of George III.

On top of everything came the discovery that the Prince of Wales had a mistress. Albert was in despair. The young man was going to be as bad as Albert's father, as Albert's brother, as Victoria's wicked uncles! The world that Albert and Stockmar had envisioned was a foolish dream. Despotism in Germany, indifference in Britain, what was there to live for?

The beautiful Coburgs did not age well. Uncle Leopold in a

One of the last photographs taken of Prince Albert, showing him in characteristic pose.

shiny black wig might have been a drawing-master; Albert, the Thuringian Siegfried, in Strachey's deadly phrase, now looked like a butler. His stomach was weak; he had violent headaches. When he came down with a fever in December 1861, at Windsor, it was first thought that it was only another of his minor ailments. But Albert knew otherwise. He told his daughter Alice, who more than any of the other children had tried to fill Vicky's place, that he was dying. He entirely accepted it. When the despairing Queen learned of this, after his death, such resignation struck her as a failure in pluck. Bitterly, she must have speculated that he had not found life worth fighting for.

On his very deathbed Albert accomplished something that seems to reverse every conclusion of this essay. All I can do is let the reader decide for himself.

Civil War in America had broken out earlier in that year. Britain had not recognized the Southern States as a nation, but she was willing to receive their envoy. Mason and Slidell, the Confederate ministers appointed to Britain and France, sailed for their posts aboard a British merchantman, the *Trent*, which was stopped on the high seas by a United States naval vessel. The diplomats were forcibly removed and taken to New York. This was a clear violation of international law, and public feeling ran high in Britain. It was just the kind of episode that Lord Palmerston, the Prime Minister, was prone to turn into a popular *casus belli*. The original draft of his dispatch sternly demanded the liberation of the individuals captured, their delivery to the British Ambassador in Washington and a full apology for the insult offered to the British flag. Fortunately, the document required royal approval. Albert dragged himself from his sickbed to work over this dangerous language and inserted the following paragraph:

Her Majesty's Government, bearing in mind the friendly relations which have long subsisted between Great Britain and the United States, are willing to believe that the United States Naval Officer who committed this aggression was not acting in compliance with any authority from his Government or that if he conceived himself to be so authorized, he greatly misunderstood the instructions which he had received.

This was followed by a polite statement trusting that the United

States would of its own accord liberate the persons captured and submit a 'suitable apology'.

Lord Palmerston's Cabinet, oddly enough, accepted the Prince's amendment, and the episode ended peaceably. If it be true that the original draft would have caused war between the two nations, Albert's place in history becomes a very important one, and his and Stockmar's efforts to enhance the authority of the Crown seem almost justified. The possible results of such a war in 1861 stagger the imagination. The Royal Navy might have destroyed the Union's blockade of the South, which might in turn have led to the election of General McClellan in 1864 and the stalemating of the Civil War. If Stockmar and Albert failed in their dream of a constitutional Germany, they may have succeeded in preserving a constitutional America.

Nine years after the settlement of the *Trent* affair, an official document in Prussia was doctored so as to create and not avoid a war. Bismarck, reading his monarch's account of an interview with the French Ambassador at Ems, saw fit to alter the language, before releasing it to the press, in such a way as to inflame popular passion on both sides. He, like Albert, accomplished exactly what he had wished.

Albert and his son Edward had almost diametrically opposite conceptions of the role of the Crown in British public life. Albert stressed the political function of the Crown, which in his day was still considerable, and he attempted to keep it within what he deemed constitutional limits. He also emphasized the role of the Crown as a patron of the arts, letters and sciences. He did not neglect the ceremonial duties, but he performed them gloomily. To Edward the latter were all-important.

Albert used to protest that his son cared for nothing but personal adornment. It is possible to see in this a son's revenge on a too strict father. What could be more odious to the exalted philosophy of the Prince Consort than the prospect of his wife's successor prancing before the public as a clothes-horse? But it is also conceivable that the son's interest in the externals of royalty, the arranging of pageants, the donning of uniforms, the seating of dinners, the correct use of orders and decorations, the whole paraphernalia of rank and precedent, reveals an instinct deeper than the father's as to what the true role of a constitutional monarch was, or at least would become.

OPPOSITE A cartoon from *Punch* 23 September 1865.

QUEEN HERMIONE.

Paulina (*Britannia*) unveils the statue.—"'Tis time! Descend; be stone no more!"

Winter's Tale, Act V., Scene 3.

_{*} Since the death of the Prince Consort, Queen Victoria had remained in almost absolute retirement. The cartoon breathes a loyal wish that her Majesty would again resume her public duties.

Edward VII, when he came to the throne after an apprentice-
ship of fifty-nine years, was in many ways a much better sovereign
than his mother. He did not interfere with his ministers, and he
implemented British foreign policy by making all the state visits
that they requested. Victoria, after Albert's death, detested and
avoided ceremonial. She hid away from her public in deep and
gloomy mourning; she refused to open or prorogue Parliament
in person, and she obliged her ministers to make constant in-
convenient journeys to Scotland for her convenience. She insisted
that she was overworked, yet she was working for the most part
on documents to which her signature was largely a formality.
She considered the political role of the sovereign to be paramount
and even pushed it to unconstitutional limits. Without the tact
and persuasiveness of Albert and later of her private secretary,
General Ponsonby, she might well have lost her crown.

The irony of the situation is that Victoria was much more
popular than her son. The reason for this must lie in the fact
that the role of royalty in the nineteenth century had become
essentially one of show or drama and that its most successful
representative had therefore to be that individual who, like a
great actor, could most effectively project a personality which
captured the imagination of an audience of subjects. An example
of how this operated is shown in the annual trips of Edward VII
and of Victoria to France. Edward went to Paris with a staff of
ten, smartly equipped and sophisticated in their knowledge of
the French and their language. Victoria travelled through France
in a private train with a household of a hundred servants to hide
away in a villa on the Riviera surrounded by a gaggle of German
relatives. Yet Edward was the one criticized for extravagance!
Presumably it was not possible for the average British subject to
put himself in the shoes of the cosmopolitan Edward, but what
housewife in Manchester or Liverpool could not picture herself
riding royally through the fair land of France without the smallest
concession to Gallicism?

It was the picture, in the last analysis, of the widow of Windsor,
acclaimed by Kipling, the small, dumpy yet incomparably royal
figure in black, with the china-blue eyes and the silvery voice,
that caught and held the imagination of the Empire. For what
was a greater proof that the Empire was virtuous, that the Empire
was kindly, that the Empire was Christian, than that it should
have as its symbol not a warlord or even a great statesman but
this little old lady who maintained the middle-class family virtues

Victoria on one of her trips to Nice on the Riviera in later life.

in the midst of a pageantry always subject to her tight control? Victoria knew what she was doing on her Diamond Jubilee when she drove with her horse guards to St Paul's Cathedral, a tiny dark controlling centre of a huge, flashing, revolving wheel. One even begins to see something deeper than jealousy in her criticism of her beautiful daughter-in-law Alexandra as a mere 'lady of society', lacking the *tenue* of a great German princess. The Crown could be a pageant, like Edward VII, but it was still better if it were a personality, like Victoria. It was Albert's tragedy that he was neither.

Chapter Three

BENJAMIN DISRAELI

riting to his friend William Dean Howells about the London literary scenes of 1881, Henry James made a withering comment about the last novel of Lord Beaconsfield, *Endymion*, which had appeared shortly before the great prime minister's death. This work of fiction had almost fatally disgusted James 'with the literary form to which it pretends to belong'. Nor was the American novelist much more enthusiastic about Disraeli the statesman. Three years previously, when war between Russia and Great Britain over the revolt of the Christian provinces in Turkey had seemed imminent, James had written to another friend: 'London smells of gunpowder, and the tawdry old Jew who is at the head of this great old British empire would like immensely to wind up his career with a fine long cannonade.'

James and Disraeli both approached British society as outsiders. One was a Yankee, the other a Jew. But James as an alien was able to present himself as a literary figure outside the hierarchy, and so not subject to being ranked by class, while Disraeli, a British subject, was always being put in his place, and a place, too, which had little enough to do with his own derisively rejected claim of being a Jewish aristocrat, grander than any peer. Both men, however, shared the romantic passion of the parvenu for the pageantry of old England. If the 'tawdry old Jew' revelled in dukes and duchesses, in diamond tiaras and prancing horse-guards, he did so no more exuberantly than the younger American novelist.

Consider the famous list of 'absent things in American life' which the expatriated James claimed, in his critical study of Hawthorne, would have had such 'an appalling effect' on a British or French imagination: 'No sovereign, no court, no personal loyalty, no aristocracy, no church, no clergy, no army, no diplomatic service, no country gentlemen, no palaces, no castles, nor manors, nor old country houses, nor parsonages, nor thatched cottages, nor ivied ruins.'

Compare this with Disraeli's description of Eton in *Coningsby*, bearing in mind that Disraeli's boyhood had been as much deprived of such elements as James's had been of his 'absent things':

That delicious plain, studded with every creation of graceful culture; hamlet and hall, and grange; garden and grove, and park; that castle-palace, grey with glorious ages; those antique spires, hoar with faith and wisdom, the chapel and the college; that river winding through the shady meads; the sunny glade and the solemn avenue; the room in the Dame's house where we first order our own breakfast and first feel we are free; the stirring multitude, the energetic groups, the individual mind that leads, conquers, controls; the emulation and the affection; the noble strife and the tender sentiment; the daring exploit and the dashing scrape; the passion that pervades our life, and breathes in everything, from the aspiring study to the inspiring sport: oh! what hereafter can spur the brain and touch the heart like this; can give us a world so deeply and variously interesting; a life so full of quick and bright excitement, passed in a scene so fair?

It certainly was and probably still is considered vulgar to admire what Disraeli admired in British life. But what was even more unforgivable than his admiration was his frank admission of it. James learned to cover up his youthful snobbery in the incomparable tapestry of his rich prose style; Disraeli never even tried. More than half a century separates the publications of *Vivian Grey* and *Endymion*, but the bedazzlement with rank is the same in each. What I continue to enjoy in Disraeli's novels is precisely this refreshing enthusiasm for the grandeur of aristocratic survivals. He simply states what millions of sentimentalists have now learned to conceal. And laugh at it all as we will, when it is all largely gone, as today, do we not feel a sneaking nostalgia for it?

The reason then, I submit, that Disraeli was loved or despised – and is still loved or despised – is that he delighted in just those aspects of imperial Britain that serious persons are supposed to mock, or at least play down. But as André Maurois astutely observed, the truly oriental side of his nature was that he could adore the material rewards of this world while still recognizing their essential nothingness.

This oriental side of Disraeli was, of course, largely assumed. His father and grandfather had been prosperous British subjects of the upper-middle class, and he himself had been admitted to the Church of England as a boy. If Henry James achieved classlessness by being a foreigner, Disraeli tried at first to achieve something like it by being an Oriental, descended, as he claimed, from the ancient and noble Lara family, who had settled in Spain. As a young dandy in London he enhanced his reputation for the exotic by publishing lurid novels and wearing gold chains and vivid colours. When he finally got into Parliament, after several unsuccessful tries, his maiden speech was interrupted with hoots of derision.

He admitted to himself at once that he had started on the wrong foot. From then on he emphasized a more British note in his dress and demeanour, although he never ceased to extol the glory of his Jewish heritage. But this last in time came to seem a harmless eccentricity. He married a rich gentile widow and bought a country estate with a Tudor-style mansion. The only foreign note was the peacocks. 'What is a terrace without them?' he would ask. But everything else in Hughenden Manor was as British as Trollope.

After his first election to the House of Commons in 1837, he retained his seat without interruption until his translation to the House of Lords, while still Prime Minister, in 1876. But in all those near forty years he held office only for six: three times as Chancellor of the Exchequer and Leader of the House, and twice as Prime Minister. This meant that the great bulk of his parliamentary career was spent in opposition, which must have intensified the unfavourable picture in the minds of many people of a carping critic, witty but malicious, who constituted a purely negative force in the business of government. Disraeli's greatest problem was that he did not offer a popular image until the very end of his career.

It was certainly not for lack of trying. Having suppressed the dandy, he promoted the image of the brooding sphinx, pale, sepulchral, immaculately garbed in black, observing all, missing nothing. This was better, but it was still not lovable. It even seemed to endorse Gladstone's theory of the Mephistophelean nature of his rival. The only thing that could save it was old age. When the sphinx became a sage, when hostility was softened by the sight of the limping old statesman clinging to the arm of his handsome and faithful secretary, Corry, when London began to ring with anecdotes of the oracle at dinner-parties, coming to life suddenly with the slashing, the perfect repartee, when it became known how the Queen and the whole royal family adored him, 'Dizzy' became nationally popular. He was now the sly, lovable

Disraeli's wife, Mary Ann, a rich Gentile widow, was twelve years his senior and adored him.

'Power and Place'. This Spy cartoon depicts Disraeli with Montague William Corry, his devoted private secretary.

Sir Robert Peel announcing his conversion to free trade principles during the Corn Law Debate in the House of Commons, 22 January 1846. Disraeli's subsequent attack on Peel brought down the Prime Minister and split the Tory party.

old wizard who was putting Britain at the helm of the world. Even Bismarck's retort shows a reluctant affection: 'The old Jew – that's the man!' The 'old' made all the difference.

Could he have done it earlier? It seems possible. His attack on Sir Robert Peel in the 1840s brought down the Prime Minister and raised Disraeli to the national attention, but the picture that lingered was of a hound with its fangs viciously locked in the neck of a noble stag. That Sir Robert should have died not long afterwards was hardly Disraeli's fault, but it may have hardened many hearts to him. A great British gentleman harried to his death by a blaspheming Jew – what a handicap to a rising politician!

Disraeli had been accused of acting out of self-interest in attacking Peel, and certainly Peel's failure to include him in the Cabinet of 1841 aroused his deep resentment, but there was still a principle at stake fundamental to Disraeli's political philosophy: party loyalty. Peel had been elected by the Tories on a protectionist promise, and now he was preparing to throw the agriculturalists to the winds in favour of importing cheap corn. Even Lord Melbourne, an easy-going moralist, called it a 'damn dishonest act'. But was it really? Peel sincerely believed that he was changing his mind for the good of Britain, and indeed free trade swept the country and ultimately carried even Disraeli along with it. Was it worth destroying the Tory party by splitting it into Peelites and Protectionists and subjecting the nation to coalition governments for the next thirty years? Suppose Disraeli had worked instead to heal the breach, suppose he had used all his famous arts of persuasion to bring Derby and Peel together, might he not have saved a great party which would have made him Prime Minister long before it did? It is true, of course, that he did make an offer to Gladstone – and a handsome one – to induce him to join Derby's Cabinet in 1858, but by then it was too late. Gladstone could never forgive the tactics which had brought Peel down.

It is difficult for us today to see the issue as a moral one, and it is difficult to believe that Disraeli did. And moving from the moral to the practical sphere, could he really have intended to split a party in order to preserve it? He seems to have been carried away by the excitement of the debate, for he must have forgotten, when he stated that he would never have agreed to serve in Peel's Cabinet, that Sir Robert was in possession not only of his letter begging for a post but of his wife's. Why Sir Robert did not use these to crush Disraeli we shall never know. Yet Disraeli's error must have been sincere, for the risk he took was otherwise a mad one. He had a habit of arranging the past to suit his own imagined convenience.

What it seems to come down to is that Disraeli was unable to resist a temptation which seemed at first blush to combine an opportunity for self-advancement with the furthering of an ostensibly great and noble cause. Peel was betraying the cause of the landed aristocracy, then championed by a group of young noblemen under Disraeli's leadership who called themselves 'Young England', in favour of the big burghers of the towns. He was not only turning on the class which Disraeli in *Coningsby*

liked at least to pretend to believe would save Britain; he was
renouncing a politically sacred commitment. What prize might
not await the David who could bring this Goliath down? Might
he not succeed Peel in a reunited party? Yes, but only thirty years
later. For what Disraeli seemed not to have foreseen was that
free trade was coming in any event, that it would soon cease to
be a moral issue, and that the person who would bear the ultimate
onus for splitting the party would be as much Disraeli as Peel.

It took a lifetime's patience to mend things, to put Humpty-
Dumpty back together again, but Disraeli did it. He gave up, for
the time, writing novels; he studied the blue books, he mastered
his figures. Perhaps the hardest job was to persuade the Protectionist leader, the Earl of Derby, that protection was a lost cause,
not only 'dead but damned'. Derby's character was immensely
frustrating to Disraeli because he was too grand to be ambitious.
He was just as happy at Knowsley translating Homer as he was
in Downing Street, and he once declined to form a government
on the Queen's urgent bid because he thought he lacked the
proper support. He did not see why it was worthwhile to jettison
even a worn-out principle to obtain power. With time and persist-
ence, however, Disraeli convinced him, but in Derby's administration it was still necessary for him to take second place, and
he did not achieve the premiership until ill health forced Derby
out of office in 1868. But, with the abandonment of protection,
Disraeli was at last free to accomplish the supreme task of his
lifetime: the creation of the first great modern political machine,
the Conservative Party.

Behind the romantic novelist was now revealed a man of iron,
a man determined, if it were humanly possible, to make Britain
fit into the framework of his dream. But in doing this he had
to be practical. He had to widen the frame; he had even to alter
the dream. What did Disraeli the statesman do for Disraeli the
novelist's euphoric ideals for 'Young England'? Very little. As
Robert Blake puts it: 'Indeed, it would have been a vain task in
the mid-nineteenth century to have solved the Condition of England question by reviving either the monarchy, the aristocracy
or the Church.' What Disraeli learned as leader of the Opposition
was that the only way that Britain could be successfully governed,
the only way that the political and social reforms necessitated by
the population increase and the industrial revolution could be
effected was by a strong party system. The party in power had
to be backed in the Commons by a disciplined majority. Ideally,

too, the Opposition should consist of a second party, equally disciplined, and ready to take over the government when the times required a change. Otherwise, nothing would ever get done.

Disraeli had no doubt himself that the reorganization of his party was his greatest achievement, and he often said so. It was also the most lasting, for the Conservatives remained the dominant party in British politics until 1960. Beside it his other accomplishments fade. The Reform Bill of 1867, important as it was, was a compromise of the suggestions of all parties. Disraeli's boast of responsibility was considered by his opponents a cheap trick. And the British Government's purchase of the Khedive's forty-four per cent interest in the Suez Canal did not, as Disraeli claimed, give Britain control of the waterway; control came only after his death with the establishment of the British protectorate of Egypt, which also rendered obsolete his policy of bolstering the Ottoman Empire against Russia's threats to the Mediterranean. This is not to minimize a great Prime Minister's achievements; it is simply to establish the order of their ultimate utility. What Disraeli understood was that he himself would never get ahead and that reform would never come until a party had been created to push both him and reform. It was a case of enlightened self-interest.

There are those, of course, who believe that Disraeli's disciplined party tended to place too much power in the Cabinet and too little in the Commons. But if one considers that the Reform Bill of 1832 enfranchised only one-seventh of the adult males of England and that the country had to wait thirty-five years for a further expansion of the vote, and if one views the long horror of neglected workers and stinking slums, I think one is forced to conclude that an organized party system was needed simply to get bills passed and not bogged down in internecine parliamentary warfare. Disraeli's dream of a Britain governed by its ancient institutions, Crown, Church and aristocracy, was hardly recognizable in its realization of a Britain governed by two parties, but the result, in terms of the franchise and the welfare of the poor, was not dissimilar.

The failure of Disraeli's maiden speech has been dramatized in many books, but I wonder if one could overdramatize its effect on his psyche. How unutterably cruel for the poet of ancient Britain, the champion of lords, to be publicly mocked in the supreme assembly of British gentlemen! Surely he must have glimpsed himself as they saw him: a vulgar, over-dressed social climber who would stop at nothing to get ahead. It was all very well for him to boast about the Laras of medieval Spain and to shrug at the titles of Cecils and Russells as dating only from the spoliation of the monasteries, but he was far too shrewd and knew London society far too well to think for a minute that anyone agreed with him.

No, the blow was cruel, but hardly a surprise. Disraeli had suffered plenty of checks before it. His early novels throb with passionate frustration and fury. The young Contarini Fleming is torn between his dreams of glory and his petty, carping relatives. 'When I contrasted my feelings and my situation I grew mad. The constant jar between my conduct and my conception was intolerable. In imagination a hero, I was in reality a boy.' Life would be unendurable unless he became the 'greatest of men'.

To the young Disraeli hero, any response to his own inner fire produced an explosion. If another young person, by a shared sympathy, seemed to be offering evidence that the beautiful world of his imagination actually existed, he would become torrid in utterance. Friendship between two men, love between a man and a woman, could be expressed in equally passionate terms. Here is how Contarini Fleming felt about his school friend, Musaeus:

On the eve of the fatal day we took our last stroll in our favourite meads. The whole way I wept, and leant upon his shoulder. With what jealous care I watched to see if he too shed a tear! One clear drop at length came quivering down his cheek, like dew upon a rose. I pardoned him for its beauty. The bell sounded. I embraced him, as if it sounded for my execution, and we parted.

It has been said that there was an element of homosexuality in Disraeli's relationships, particularly later in life, with young men. Did he care about his handsome aide, Montague Corry, as he cared for Lady Bradford? Possibly. But I suspect that his feelings for both were less intense than his demonstrative expressions might lead one to suspect. Writers who talk in hyperbolic terms of passion do not necessarily have correspondingly deep feelings, and there was a fundamental coolness in Disraeli's nature. He loved the idea of ardour, of beauty, of power, of mystery. The English went in for passionate friendships in their public schools for which they made up with a lifetime of coolness. Love for a youth was normally followed by love for a girl; the Victorians did not use our pigeonholes. Contarini planned to consummate his love for Musaeus by a sexual union with the latter's sister:

He was to be my heart's friend from the beginning to the death. And I mourned that nature had given me no sister, with whom I could bind him to me by a still stronger and sweeter tie. And then, with a shy, hesitating voice, for he delighted not in talking of his home, he revealed to me that he was more blessed; and Caroline Musaeus rose up once to me like a star, and without having seen her I was indeed her betrothed.

One is reminded here of Arthur Hallam's engagement to Emily Tennyson.

Disraeli always liked to cultivate the appearances of love. Only in his early affair with Henrietta Sykes does there seem to have been a note of real passion, and even there one senses that he was rather uneasy, almost relieved to have it over and done with. Having never, apparently, been congenial with his mother, he sought and evoked maternal feelings in older women. His wife, Mary Ann, twelve years his senior, adored him, fussed over him, boasted about him, quoted him. Queen Victoria was always begging him to take care of himself. Mrs Brydges Willyams could think of nothing better to do with her large residuary estate than bequeath it to him.

Yet he was perfectly sincere with all of them. The trouble that some observers have in interpreting Disraeli is that they assume that he must have meant his hyperbole literally or not at all. But this need not have been the case. He loved Mary Ann; he even, in his way, loved the Queen, but it amused him to express his affections in much stronger terms than required by conventional usage. A good stout middle-class British suspicion that all such effusions are 'phony' need not be more than half accurate. The women of Disraeli's era appreciated his gallantry in dressing up a mild emotion, in putting it, so to speak, in party clothes.

Mary Ann was just as vulgar as he was – more so. One wonders if a real gentleman and lady would have agreed, as they did, to hang on to the husband's seat in the House of Commons, without forfeiting a peerage, by the simple expedient of having the latter honour conferred on the wife. Gladstone (why did people say he had no humour?) observed, when Disraeli persuaded the Queen to ennoble his private secretary, Montague Corry, that there had been nothing like it since Caligula had made his horse

The Countess of Bradford, for whom Disraeli conceived a great affection which she constantly urged him to moderate.

a consul. He was probably too gallant to make the same gibe against Mary Ann, of whom, oddly enough, he was always very fond. That Mary Ann loved being a viscountess as much as her husband would later delight in being an earl is shown in a letter of William Cory to Lord Esher: 'He [Lord Rosebery] showed me today a strange skewer scrawl of Lady Beaconsfield's with the vulgarest big B under her glaring coronet, and her initial lost in the Beaconsfield of the signature, so that you would take her for a male.'

There was one inamorata, however, the last, who was always pulling Disraeli up. Lady Bradford and her sister, Lady Chesterfield, occupied most of the old man's emotional life after the death of Mary Ann. Lady Chesterfield was Disraeli's contemporary, and it was she who received and turned down his proposal of marriage, probably because she suspected that he was only seeking to be closer to her younger sister, who was possessed of a perfectly good husband. Lady Bradford was thus placed in a difficult position. On the one hand it was pleasant to be the favourite of the Prime Minister, the most famous man in England, and the recipient of fascinating state secrets (he told her about the Suez purchase before it was public). On the other, the old man's indiscretions (he was as loose with his compliments as with the confidences of his Cabinet) could be embarrassing and possibly of real annoyance to her husband. Some writers have believed that her rebuffs, her placing a limit on his visits, caused real agony to her aged lover. But I suspect that he rather enjoyed the game. 'I live for Power and the affections,' he wrote to her, 'and one may enjoy both without being bored and wearied with all the dull demands of conventional intercourse.' Or again: 'To see you, or, at least, to hear from you every day, is absolutely necessary to my existence, or, rather, if these conditions were wanting, there would be a change in the order of my life which would astonish the world.'

Of course, at moments she could hurt him. The difference in their ages made this inevitable. There is a note of real pain in the following, received the day after she has refused to be monopolized by him at a ball: 'Your feelings to me are not the same as mine have been to you. That is natural and reasonable. Mine make me sensitive and perhaps exigent, and render my society in public embarrassing to you.' Nobody, after all, likes to be made to feel ridiculous. But for the most part he flourished happily enough with the pantomime of love. 'I must say that I feel fortunate in having a female sovereign,' he confessed to her. 'I owe everything to woman; and if in the sunset of life I have still a young heart, it is due to that influence.'

The writer in Disraeli could be counted on in the long run to describe the exact role of love in his life, and here is what he told Lady Bradford in 1874:

But when you have the government of a country on your shoulders, to love a person and to be in love with a person makes all the difference. In the first case everything that distracts your mind from your great purpose weakens and wearies you. In the second instance the difficulty of seeing your beloved or communicating with her, only animates and excites you.

So it was fun, after all.

Queen Victoria was forty-nine during Disraeli's brief first tenure as Prime Minister and fifty-five at the beginning of his second. She had long been a widow, and her figure had rounded. It is possible that there existed an element of sexual attraction in her devotion to the rough, bluff gillie, John Brown, who treated her with an outrageous and titillating familiarity and who was reputed to spike her tea with whisky, but it is less likely that there was any such emotion in her friendship for the gouty and cadaverous statesman fourteen years her senior. Disraeli's secret was not sex; he simply made the business of ruling a romance.

It is always said that he flattered her, and he did so, unblushingly. His letters to her are sickening in their sweetness. But there was nothing feigned about the rhapsody that he himself felt when his compliments were returned. Lady Bradford was made a daily witness to the manifestations of the royal grace: 'The Faery sent for me the instant I arrived. I can only describe my reception by telling you that I really thought she was going to embrace me. She was wreathed with smiles, and as she talked, glided about the room like a bird.' The Queen even asked him to be seated! Previous to this, he gleefully explained, her greatest condescension had been to express her regret to the gout-stricken Lord Derby that etiquette forbade her to offer him a chair.

What is much less clear, however, is the extent to which his flattery affected the Queen. She enjoyed it, to be sure, for Disraeli had the imagination to use slightly subtler terms than the ones habitually used to sovereigns. But she must have been at least

Tom Merry, del. et lith.

partially inured to the jargon of courtly compliments. If she appreciated a change in style, as she might have appreciated a dash of whisky in her tea, she was hardly going to alter her conduct as monarch for it. A perusal of her correspondence with her favourite minister makes it quite evident that when she really wanted something, no amount of persuasiveness, no matter how sugared, would talk her out of it. Only when she detected the looming shadow of a constitutional impasse would she yield. But then she did. Her basic common sense was like a rock.

She had not at first approved of Disraeli. He had savaged her adored Sir Robert Peel, and Albert thought he was not a gentleman. When Disraeli first came to office, she insisted that Lord Derby, then premier, be responsible to keep him in hand as leader of the House of Commons. But Albert thawed as he came to know the new Chancellor of the Exchequer, and Disraeli, after the Prince's death, scored heavily with the widow in his lavish tributes to the deceased. And then his reports to the sovereign, as leader of the House, were so entrancing! Just like his novels, the Queen thought. Where Albert had made business so heavy that she was glad to leave it to him, Disraeli made one want to join in it. As Prime Minister he never dropped the pretence that she was the real ruler, he only the adviser. Gladstone thought that he did a disservice to the Constitution in giving the Queen an inflated idea of her powers, but I believe that she had that anyway, and we shall see how Disraeli handled her when she went too far.

To the widowed Queen all Albert's tenets were sacred. He had conceived the constitutional monarch, in Stockmar's ideology, as a kind of permanent premier, with very real powers. The duty of that monarch was to exercise those powers wisely, and to do so he had to know every proposed act of Parliament, every regulation, every treaty, to the bottom. The Queen was resolved to tackle the work-load that had fallen from her deceased husband's shoulders, no matter what the consequences to her health. But in return for what she deemed her own heroic self-sacrifice, she stipulated that she be relieved of all social and ceremonial duties. To do the job that nobody asked of her, she would give up the job that everyone expected of her. She would live and labour in sepulchral isolation, *except* that she required an absolute freedom to go to Balmoral or Osborne, or to visit her German relatives whenever she chose, regardless of the inconvenience to her ministers.

OPPOSITE Victoria was totally won over by Disraeli, and even visited him at his house, Hughenden, in Buckinghamshire, an event which attracted considerable attention in the press.

It was small wonder that the Queen lost so much of her popularity in the 1860s. Her conception of her own role was now precisely the opposite of her subjects'. Instead of a splendid figurehead presiding over a pageant, they saw an evasive, self-pitying little woman in ugly black hiding away behind castle walls to fuss with papers that she probably shouldn't be reading at all! Under the circumstances a republican government began to seem cheaper and more efficient to many.

Disraeli understood all this. He saw that it was essential to change the Queen's view of her role, and he saw that that could be done only by persuasion, even by coaxing. He had to make the business of government attractive. For the Crown, certainly, was essential to his conception of the Constitution. It is more difficult to determine just what he considered the extent of its authority should be. It seems likely that he believed that the sovereign should have wide powers, vaguely defined, but should rarely, if ever, exercise them, and that it was the job of the Prime Minister to keep this situation constantly in hand. The whole thing was like a theatrical production; the director had to have a watchful eye on each step, each gesture, each speech, each chorus. But that was what a director was for, was it not? If he couldn't do it, the House of Commons should oust him. We shall return to this metaphor again.

Queen Victoria, despite a deportment and demeanour that all observers describe as incomparably royal, had many middle-class characteristics, which may have accounted for much of her great, later popularity. She was down-to-earth, shrewd, sceptical, candid and scrupulously honest. She lived in a clutter of memorabilia, of each item of which she had a housekeeper's awareness, and she exerted a taut control over her nine children and almost innumerable grandchildren. She maintained a staggering correspondence, pouring forth her comments to the royalties of Europe on her health, her pets, her walks, her drives, her weather – as well as on events that shook the world. Inevitably, to one living so long on so high an altitude, the proportions had to blur: a grandchild's cough, a royal visit, the death of a dog, an imperial assassination, a plague, an earthquake, a war, fell into their places as parts of the royal day. And she also had a strong middle-class taste for the most saccharin kind of drama. It was not difficult for Disraeli, with a little patience, to dramatize her to herself.

When one reads how much she troubled him, one can appreciate the problems of the less loved prime ministers. The Queen

was fervently devoted to Disraeli, and grateful for the pleasure which she derived from her sessions with him, but as with other women he brought out the maternal in her. She fussed over his health, deplored his solitary life, sent him flowers and choice foods, in short, clucked over him. She was jealous of his popularity with her own children and tended to pout when he visited her son at Sandringham. But where the maternal feelings were most troublesome was in her determination that he needed to be pushed. If he regarded her as a 'faery' to be cajoled and manipulated, she regarded him as an amiable old darling who might be hoodwinked by the blackguard Russian Czar whom she knew better than he! The curious truth is that each condescended a bit to the other. The Queen did not really believe that the author of *Tancred* could basically understand the appointment of her middle-of-the-road candidates to the Church of England, and he described privately her wish to intervene personally to settle a dispute between the two Houses of Parliament as a 'child's scheme'. The fact that each believed that he or she had to help the other intensified their friendship.

Disraeli could be unctuous and wheedling: he lent himself to the *Punch* caricatures which showed him as a smiling, hand-rubbing oriental merchant of questionable wares. Anyone, even a sovereign, who thought that he could be controlled

The Queen lived in a clutter of memorabilia, as this photograph of her sitting-room at Balmoral Castle shows. She often had to be coaxed away from the past by a tactful Disraeli to deal with affairs of state.

soon learned his error. Disraeli, as I have said, was like a stage director. What actor or actress has not heard that soft, that sometimes purring voice from the auditorium, with all those 'dears' and 'darlings', and not recognized the latent tone of command as sharp as any in a military barracks? The Prime Minister adored great plays, great sets, great roles, but he gave short shrift to those who forgot their lines or stepped out of character. A princess of the royal house asked him, in a time of political crisis, to call on her at a quarter to ten in the morning. 'Had I been as idle as a ploughboy sitting on a gate,' he told a friend, 'I would not have gone. A liberty to ask me to derange my day for such a frivolity!' And the Queen herself, urging him to receive Lord Chelmsford at Hughenden, received this firm, even stern refusal:

Lord Beaconsfield charges Lord Chelmsford with having invaded Zululand *avec un cœur léger* with no adequate knowledge of the country he was attacking and no precaution or preparation ... It is most painful for Lord Beaconsfield to differ from Your Majesty in any view of public affairs, not merely because he is bound to Your Majesty by every tie of duty and respectful affection, but because he has a distinct and real confidence in Your Majesty's judgment, matured, as it is, by an unrivalled political experience, and an extensive knowledge of mankind.

What is this but a hint to the Faery that she had better restudy her part? Imperial pageantry might have been fun, but she who played the queen was, in the last analysis, only another member of the cast. The rule applied to all. 'Don't talk to me of dukes,' Disraeli once snorted. 'Dukes can be made.'

  The security of real power enabled Disraeli to relax some of his vigil and enjoy himself during his second and final ministry (1874–80). He was sixty-nine at the start, almost crippled with gout, harassed by bronchitis, and he bitterly missed the cheerful companionship of the beloved Mary Ann who had died four years before. Indeed, it looked, as he himself complained, as if the great prize had come too late. But there were good things, too. The Queen, who had sorely regretted the fall from power of this enchanting vizier after the ten months' ministry of 1868, made no secret of her delight in having him back. The Conservative Party, united at last, with a good majority, offered the prospect of a solid term of office. Lady Bradford and Lady Chesterfield were there to stimulate the 'affections'. And finally, the crisis in the Middle East created by Russia's attack on the Ottoman Empire, allegedly to protect the Christian minorities but actually

OPPOSITE Windsor Castle, like all the royal residences, came under the stern scrutiny of Prince Albert. He soon brought order to the disorganized chaos of the royal household.

OVERLEAF: ABOVE LEFT The South Front of Hughenden Manor, Disraeli's home.

BELOW LEFT Disraeli's study, Hughenden Manor.

RIGHT Disraeli by Sir Francis Grant.

OPPOSITE Sir Edwin Landseer's painting 'Windsor Castle in Modern Times', showing Victoria and Albert with Vicky, the Princess Royal, in the early 1840s. Albert is portrayed sitting with his dogs and the game which he has shot, while his demure wife stands beside him.

to gain a foothold in the Mediterranean, offered a theatre of operations for which his long preoccupation with Arab and Semitic affairs seemed peculiarly to have fitted him. Truly, the dream had come true. His hero, Tancred, was Prime Minister of England! If the nation would not go into a novel, a novel might take over the nation.

It was hard work, of course. He underestimated the feeling aroused in Britain by the Bulgarian atrocities committed by the Turks, a feeling which Gladstone took care to blow into a high flame. While coping with those who were almost ready to go to war with Turkey to save the Christians, he had to restrain the Queen, who was passionately anxious to fight the Russians and who peppered him with memoranda calling for a more belligerent stand: 'Oh, if the Queen were a man, she would like to give those Russians, whose word one cannot believe, such a beating! We shall never be friends again till we have it out.' A third group, which included three members of his own Cabinet, wanted England to do nothing. The harassed premier, who was playing what a later American diplomat was to call 'brinksmanship', was determined to keep Russia out of Constantinople by measures short of war, and he succeeded in the end in doing so despite all the fury of the press and all the threats of abdication and resignation. The Congress of Berlin in 1878 made him the

Victoria kept up a staggering correspondence with the royalties of Europe, particularly her eldest daughter, Vicky.

On 1 May 1876, Victoria was proclaimed Empress of India. In this cartoon she is presented with the crown of India in exchange for the British crown, by a simpering Oriental Disraeli.

"NEW CROWNS FOR OLD ONES!"

first statesman of Europe, and his return to London was celebrated by a popular ovation.

But perhaps the moment when life and fiction seemed most to blend was that when he toasted his sovereign by her new title as Empress of India. He had had trouble in Parliament with the Royal Titles Bill, and the press had had a field-day, but nothing could spoil the dinner at Windsor which Lord George Hamilton has described in his memoirs. The Queen, usually so homely in attire, appeared in 'a mass of oriental jewelry, mostly consisting of very large uncut stones and pearls', gifts from the reigning princes of India. The newly created Earl of Beaconsfield broke etiquette by proposing the health of the new Empress 'with a little speech as flowing as the oration of a Maharajah', to which the Queen responded with a pretty, smiling bow, half a curtsy.

A bit too much? A silly, an almost grotesque, pantomime with a fat little middle-aged woman playing the oriental despot and the jaded old conjurer grinning up his sleeve but still enjoying it? Was it a parody of empire, a mockery of the grinding of hundreds of millions of people under the sway of this grimacing, fantasizing couple? Did they make the Empire glorious or ridiculous? Did they misrepresent the British spirit totally (as Gladstone would have maintained) or were they of its essence? *Was* the Empire tawdry, vulgar? Or was there something inspiring in the pomp and circumstance, the spirit, the courage, the red coats?

Whatever side one comes down on, one has to admit that Disraeli did his best to dress up the British state. There are times today when one may almost miss the great decorator.

Disraeli the novelist survives through Disraeli the statesman. Without his political career the books would be quite forgotten. Even the two most read today, *Coningsby* and *Sybil*, enunciate a political theory which would seem simply quaint if it had not once been the credo of 'Young England', that band of youthful aristocratic politicians who in the 1840s had rallied behind Disraeli in an effort to wrest the body politic from the Whigs and the industrialists and return it to the control of a renovated class system. Yet Disraeli himself thought very highly of his works, which he described as his 'life', and expected his friends to read them all. Unfavourable critics he described as frustrated novelists, and he subjected Thackeray, who had once published a howlingly funny burlesque of *Coningsby*, to a cruel satire in *Endymion*, years after the great author's death.

Why, it may be asked, is it at all surprising that Disraeli should have suffered from the vanity common to authors? Because so much of his fiction is so extraordinarily bad that one wonders he did not see it himself. It seems curious that a man who was capable of such remarkable patience and self-control should have eschewed all discipline in writing novels. He simply allows his imagination to follow its natural course: *Vivian Grey* and *Contarini Fleming* degenerate from picaresque novels into travelogues, and the hero of *Tancred*, searching for the answer to the problems of modern European civilization and wafted by

The familiar aspect of
Disraeli, deliberately
cultivated, as the sober
man impeccably dressed
in black, from a portrait
by Sir John Everett
Millais.

the plot from London to the Holy Land, is carried to the peak of
Mount Sinai where he has a vision of an angel and hears a voice
crying: 'Theocratic equality.' There is no development of character and, indeed, very little character; there is simply melodrama,
some mildly amusing dialogue and a great many descriptions of
lavish parties and fabulous castles which end with the author's
asking the reader to accept them for what they are supposed to
be, as in the following: 'But the scene was brilliant: a marvellous
lawn, the Duchess's Turkish tent with its rich hangings, and the
players themselves, the prettiest of all the spectacle, with their
coquettish hats, and their half-veiled and half-revealed under-
raiment, scarlet and silver, or blue and gold, *made up a sparkling
and modish scene.* (Italics added)

One might think that Disraeli's style could not be burlesqued,
but Thackeray in *Codlingsby* proved otherwise. Here is Miriam
de Mendoza, whose arm was whiter 'than the ivory grand piano
on which it leaned':

As Miriam de Mendoza greeted the stranger, turning upon him the
solemn welcome of her eyes, Codlingsby swooned almost in the
brightness of her beauty. It was well she spoke; the sweet kind voice
restored him to consciousness. Muttering a few words of incoherent
recognition, he sank upon a sandalwood settee, as Goliath, the little
slave, brought aromatic coffee in cups of opal, and alabaster spittoons,
and pipes of the fragrant Gibelly.

'My lord's pipe is out,' said Miriam with a smile, remarking the
bewilderment of her guest – who in truth forgot to smoke – and taking
up a thousand-pound note from a bundle on the piano, she lighted
it at the taper and proceeded to re-illumine the extinguished chibouk
of Lord Codlingsby.

But still there are delightful passages in the novels, enough to
make one sorrow that the writer never mastered this trade. The
plotting of Cardinal Grandison and the priests to bring the hero
of *Lothair* into the Church of Rome, the rebellion of Coningsby
from the dominion of his despotic grandfather, the assault on
Mowbray castle by the Chartist mob in *Sybil*, all belong in better
books. And Disraeli's handling of the 'great world' is sure. This
one-sentence characterization of Lord Monmouth is worthy of
Thackeray, who used the same model (the Marquess of Hertford)
for Lord Steyne in *Vanity Fair*: 'Lord Monmouth – whose contempt for mankind was absolute; not a fluctuating sentiment, not
a mournful conviction, ebbing and flowing with circumstances,
but a fixed, profound, unalterable instinct; who never loved

anyone, and never hated anyone except his own children – was diverted by his popularity, but he was also gratified by it.'

Sometimes, too, there are descriptions, usually of great country estates, which give much the same pleasure as looking through a big Victorian album of romantic prints. This is from *Lothair*:

It was an Italian palace of freestone; vast, ornate, and in scrupulous condition; its spacious and graceful chambers filled with treasures of art, and rising itself from statued and stately terraces. At their foot spread a gardened domain of considerable extent, bright with flowers, dim with coverts of rare shrubs, and musical with fountains. Its limit reached a park, with timber such as the midland counties only can produce. The fallow deer trooped among its ferny solitudes and gigantic oaks; but beyond the waters of the broad and winding lake the scene became more savage, and the eye caught the dark form of the red deer on some jutting mount, shrinking with scorn from communion with his gentler brethren.

Disraeli may have used his novels as a means of indulging the fantasizing side of his imagination which had so little scope in politics until the very end, when he could settle the fate of the gorgeous East in Berlin. Certainly, the dry statistics of the Exchequer, the infinite complications of a franchise based on rents, on ratings, on freeholds, on deposits, on everything, evidently, but humanity, the long drill of party discipline and the eternal mess of Ireland, all against a seeming lifetime on the front bench of Opposition, were a far cry from the romantic dreams of Contarini Fleming and Tancred. But if there was a touch of Byron's Corsair behind the grave and sphinx-like Prime Minister, so was there something of the ward politician in the exuberant romancer. Sir Henry Ponsonby, the Queen's private secretary, saw this clearly.

I so fully believe that Disraeli really has an admiration for splendour, for Duchesses with ropes of pearls, for richness and gorgeousness, mixed I also think with a cynical sneer and a burlesque thought about them. When he formed the Government, he spoke in the highest delight of the great names he had selected for the household offices and the minor offices – 'sons of great Dukes'. His speech here on the Palatial Grandeur, the Royal Physician who attended on him, the Royal footmen who answered his beck and nod, the rich plate, etc – all was worked up half really, half comically into an expression of admiration for Royalty and the Queen. Yet there might also have been a sarcasm under it all.

There certainly was.

Chapter Four

SIR HENRY PONSONBY

The position of private secretary to the sovereign originated surprisingly late, for it was not until 1805 that Sir Herbert Taylor was appointed as such assistant to the ageing and near-lunatic George III. Custom had previously required that the monarch should indicate his pleasure only through his constitutional advisers in the Privy Council, and the Secretary of State for Home Affairs had been accountable for the King's correspondence. When Sir Herbert's appointment was terminated by the definite insanity of the King and the establishment of a regency, the office lapsed. The Prince of Wales, as regent and later as king, had secretaries, but they were not called that, and they were paid out of his private funds. Unhappily, they made fortunes in office, and even the good work of the faithful Sir Herbert, who was recreated private secretary to William IV, could not dispel the prejudice against a position which in the eyes of Parliament was now a source of corruption and a danger to Cabinet secrecy. Because of this sentiment, Lord Melbourne advised the young Queen Victoria not to renew the office. He solved the problem by acting as her secretary himself.

After Melbourne's fall, Baroness Lehzen, the Queen's old governess, became the *de facto* private secretary and remained so until replaced by Prince Albert. The latter continued in the office until his death, if one can call a 'private secretary' the person who was in charge in everything. When in 1861 General Charles Grey, son of the Whig Prime Minister, became private secretary *de jure* to the stricken widow, nobody ventured to criticize the restoration of so obviously necessary an office. Grey remained in the post until his death in 1870, when he was succeeded by Henry Ponsonby, his wife's nephew-in-law.

Ponsonby was the most charming type of English gentleman of his epoch. If they had all been like him, Kipling's 'lesser breeds without the law' might have clamoured for admission to the Empire. He was quiet, witty, cultivated and shrewd, a brave soldier with a gentle manner, possessed of a deep and sympathetic

PREVIOUS PAGE Sir Henry Ponsonby, Victoria's private secretary for thirty years.

understanding of the idiosyncrasies and perversities of human nature. He was an aristocrat, a nephew of the Earl of Bessborough and of Lady Caroline Lamb, but as the son of a younger son he was obliged to support himself by either a military or a clerical career. He chose the army and was sent to Ireland as ADC to the Lord Lieutenant, then his uncle, Lord Bessborough. It was probably in Dublin, during the royal visit of 1853, that he first attracted the notice of Prince Albert. Thereafter he was sent out to fight in the Crimea, and when he returned, the Prince, who never forgot anything or anyone, appointed him as his equerry.

He was the perfect aide. He moved with ease and composure among the great, always tactful and even-tempered. He understood all gradations of rank, without being unduly impressed by it. Order and precedence were simply part of his everyday business. He was as British as Palmerston, but more attractively – polite, considerate, eminently fair. He liked to work out problems, and he knew that the machinery of monarchy had to work smoothly if it was to work at all. It was a business where details could never be ignored. As in a stage production, every gesture, every costume, every prop, every light counted for the final effect. Ponsonby would have approved the courtier's retort to Philip II when the Spanish monarch chafed at some 'idle' ceremony: 'Sire, you yourself are a ceremony.' Albert, at any rate, was no Philip II. He knew as well as Ponsonby the value of forms.

To what extent did Ponsonby believe in the royal system? It is hard to say. He and his wife, the former Mary Bulteel, who had been a lady-in-waiting to the Queen, were both liberals in politics and had alert, questioning minds. They were exact observers, and nothing that was ludicrous in Court circles missed their probe, as we know from the long letters which they exchanged while he was at Balmoral and she remained with the children at Windsor. But beneath their laughter there seems to have been a considerable affection not only for the monarch but for the monarchy. At least on his part. Ponsonby was a loyal soldier, and the sovereign was his commander-in-chief. Mary was loyal to him. Left to herself, one suspects that she might have been more critical.

After Albert's death there could be no question of abandoning the forlorn widow, and Ponsonby was committed to a Court career so long as he was needed. In 1870 he was promoted to the post of private secretary, which he held until his death twenty-five years later. It is generally conceded that he raised the job to a great art. He based it on a remarkable understanding of his royal mistress. Ponsonby noted her best and her worst qualities without falling into the pitfalls of adulation or disapproval. He recognized that the Queen could be both utterly charming and utterly exasperating, and that it was up to him to complement her volatility by being always the same: grave, sympathetic, deeply courteous, with a small smile ready, either for the moment when *she* smiled – or when she did not. So vividly does the figure of Victoria emerge from the material compiled by his son Arthur in *Henry Ponsonby: His Life from his Letters* that I should mark that volume to be saved if I could save only one from the vast library of books dealing with the Queen, and I say this in no denigration of the splendid contributions of Lytton Strachey, Elizabeth Longford and Cecil Woodham-Smith.

When Ponsonby first became private secretary, the Queen was at the low point of her popularity. The public did not see why nine years was not long enough for such black mourning, and they were beginning to wonder if she ever meant to resume her public functions. Victoria resented this deeply. She felt that she was doing quite enough for her people if she spent long, gruelling hours at her desk reviewing (far more than they wanted) the decisions of her Cabinet, and that it was unreasonable and even cruel of them to expect a bereaved widow to put herself on public parade. The Prime Minister, Mr Gladstone, gave her good advice, but too much of it; he only intensified her resistance. Her children, her ladies, the whole Court were too much in awe of her to oppose her will. The older generation, which might have stood up to her, had disappeared with the Duchess of Kent. There was only the private secretary, and his political opinions were suspect to the royal view. It was true, of course, that he had fought bravely in the Crimea and that he had married dear Mary Bulteel, but was he not a Whig, a liberal and, worse still, an admirer of the dreadful Gladstone? And wasn't even dear Mary the least bit radical? Oh, yes, the Ponsonbys were still on approval. One unguarded remark about the royal isolation, and they might be looking for another position.

Ponsonby, who was determined to help the Queen, even in spite of herself, devised what his son was to call the 'Ponsonby method', which was to act as a moderator between the sovereign's will and those destined to feel the brunt of it, sometimes softening its expression at the source, sometimes screening it, only as a last resort attempting to deflect it.

There were occasions when the Queen's decisions could be altered simply by going along with them. Ponsonby would cheerfully acquiesce, and then, as if by way of parenthesis, with a kind of shrug, he might drop a hint of minor disadvantages, in the nature of eggs broken to make omelettes. If, for example, the Queen did not want to take any housemaids on a particular excursion, well, fine and good. Ponsonby would arrange for local help, but would Her Majesty please not leave her valuables about to tempt strangers? Or if the Queen requested Ponsonby to ask a Cabinet officer not to write her 'irritating letters' while she was unwell, he would agree to comply, but in so doing he might let drop the hint of an excuse for the minister's conduct in the recent Press attacks upon the Cabinet for keeping 'Your Majesty in the dark'.

Sometimes the tensions could be reduced and a crisis averted simply by softening the royal language. Here is how he handled a letter on army reform from Sir Garnet Wolseley to the Queen in which the General had the misfortune to cite the late Prince Consort in support of his proposals. The Queen sent this angry minute to Ponsonby:

This is a shameless & shameful letter. Pray take advantage of what he says abt the Pce whose name he takes in vain to say that you know that *many* of the changes made wd have been most highly disapproved of by him & that the short service ws almost universally admitted to be ruin to the efficiency of the army.

Ponsonby 'took advantage' of what Wolseley had said by addressing the following to him, adding invented congratulations on his South African campaign:

I have to return you many thanks for your letter which contained so many references to subjects of importance that I considered myself at liberty to show it to the Queen who read it with very great interest. The Queen was sincerely glad when she received some time ago the news of your successful operations against Sikukuni's fort, and your account of the operations on that occasion and of the conduct of the troops gave her very great pleasure indeed. . . .

Nothing is being done about Army reform as we are all waiting for the report of the Commission. But I think I ought to let you know that the allusions in your letter to short service, implying that the Prince Consort was favourable to that system, did not meet with the Queen's entire approbation.

Nobody was more aware than Ponsonby of the danger to the Crown of the Queen's continued retirement. He saw that she had her doctor, Sir William Jenner, completely under her thumb, that he could be counted on to prescribe against the least exertion that was contrary to her wishes. The Queen could dance at the Gillies' Ball at Balmoral from ten till two in the morning; she could walk or drive for miles in the chilly air of the Scottish Highlands, but she was far too delicate to hold a levee in London or to open or prorogue Parliament. But Ponsonby knew that direct advice would be both resented and ignored. There was nothing to be done but to watch and take advantage of the smallest crumbling in her defences.

There were moments, however, when the secretary had to place himself in direct opposition to his mistress. It was bad enough that the Queen should hide herself away from her public, but it would be much worse if she should present herself, through her own authorship, in too glaring a public light. This threatened to be the case when she announced her proposal to write a life of the adored gillie, John Brown, who had died, unregretted by the Court but very bitterly mourned by the Queen, in 1883. A biography by the royal hand would tend to confirm the worst suspicions of those who already referred to their sovereign as 'Mrs Brown'.

Leaves from a Highland Journal, the Queen's account of her daily life in Scotland, had been a very different story. Indeed, it might have been regarded as royalist propaganda. As Arthur Ponsonby amusingly puts it:

The publication of *Leaves from the Highlands* and *More Leaves* which had an enormous circulation was of great assistance to her, not that there was the smallest deliberate intention on her part to delude the public. Whatever the merits or demerits of these volumes may be, they present an innocent and rather sentimental picture of purely domestic events, expeditions, family goings and comings, little ceremonies, country scenes and deaths, births and marriages. It would not require much research, however, to pick out a date recording some colourless, unimportant incident and to find in her correspondence on the same day some letter to the Prime Minister or the Private Secretary expressing in her most vehement language her desire to interfere in high matters of national importance.

John Brown, the faithful gillie to whom Victoria clung for comfort after the death of Albert. Painting by Kenneth MacLeay.

Yet, despite this, the Prince of Wales expressed doubts as to the propriety of publishing *More Leaves*, which provoked this frigid minute from the Queen to her secretary: 'It is very strange

Sir William Jenner was the Queen's doctor and was completely under her control. He would recommend that she rest whenever it suited her to do so.

that objection should come from that quarter where great strictness as to conduct is not generally much cared for.'

Sir Henry used all the processes of indirection to quash the Brown biography. He tried repeatedly to persuade the Queen that someone else should be commissioned to write the book, but when all else had failed, he resorted to a direct appeal:

But as Sir Henry proceeds he becomes more bold and asks the Queen's forgiveness if he expresses a doubt whether this record of Your Majesty's innermost and most sacred feelings should be made public to the world. There are passages which will be misunderstood if read by strangers and there are expressions which will attract remarks of an unfavourable nature towards those who are praised; and Sir Henry cannot help fearing that the feeling created by such a publication would become most distressing and painful to the Queen.

The project was abandoned, and as usual in the rare cases of royal concession, never mentioned again. But the greatest danger of all – the one beside which all else paled – was that the Queen would one day go too far in exercising the royal prerogative in the choice of her ministers. The young unmarried monarch who had caused a constitutional crisis by refusing to exchange her Whig ladies for Tories when Sir Robert Peel had toppled the Melbourne government was still very much present in the middle-

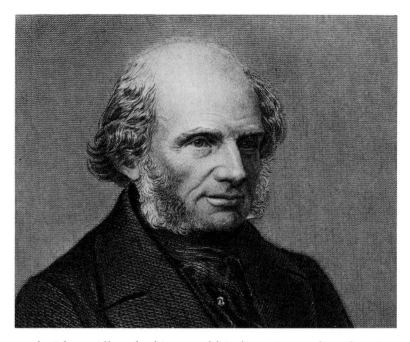

Lord John Russell, one of the 'two terrible old men' (the other was Palmerston) whose premiership Victoria grudgingly endured.

aged widow. Albert had imposed his discretion and moderation upon her, and the Crown had been secure while he lived, but his belief in the power of the sovereign had been much the same as hers (both emanating from Stockmar), and without his shrewd, practical sense of when to be assertive and when to submit, the Queen seemed headed for trouble. Indeed, she might have been more in danger of her own nature as a widow than as a maid, for she had now canonized the dead man's credo and could have been tempted to abdicate rather than give up the least of what the sacred Albert had deemed her inviolate rights.

So long as Victoria had a prime minister of whom she approved, the situation could be kept in hand. After Albert's death she had Lord Palmerston and Lord John Russell, those 'two terrible old men', venerable figures whose ability she had at last grudgingly learned to recognize, Lord Derby, whose party she liked, and Disraeli, whom she adored. But from the very beginning of Gladstone's first administration in 1869 things had gone poorly between them. He handled crowds better than individuals, and the Queen understandably objected to being treated as a crowd. Unfortunately, her objections waxed hotter with time until at last they reached almost psychopathic proportions. Here are samples,

The State Apartments of Windsor Castle, where Victoria and Albert spent their honeymoon.

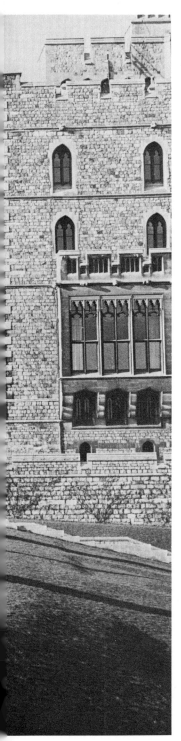

selected at random over the years, of her comments to Ponsonby:

The great alarm in the country is Mr Gladstone, the Queen perceives, and she will sooner *abdicate* than send for or have any *communication* with that *half-mad fire brand* who would soon ruin everything and be a *Dictator* ... He [Sir Henry] says 'Mr Gladstone is *loyal and devoted to the Queen*'!!! He is *neither* ... How can Mr Gladstone at seventy-six with a broken voice stand again? ... This [a Gladstone speech] is so monstrous and wicked that the Queen wishes Sir Henry to try and see someone who can speak the truth to Mr Gladstone ... But the Queen and many *still hope* the Queen and *the country* may not be exposed to such a misfortune as to be in the hands of such dangerous and reckless people as Mr Gladstone and his crew ... Though she supposes she will have that dangerous old fanatic thrust down her throat, she thinks she would like to see Lord Rosebery first when the time comes, as she must have security for [the] Foreign Office ... In the Queen's heart (and in that of many others she knows) she holds *Mr Gladstone responsible* by imprudence, neglect, violent language, for the lives of many thousands, though unwittingly ... How she prays he may give up – for he is insufferable, arguing and never listening to anything said against his *own wise notions. It is unbearable* ... The Queen cannot make up her mind to send at once for that dreadful old man.

This antipathy lasted until Gladstone's final retirement in 1894, an event which the Queen greeted with undisguised relief. It has been said that she was jealous of him; it seems quite probable. He was the only prime minister of her reign to achieve a massive popular following, indeed the only one to cultivate it. He became a kind of god in his lifetime; he seemed to threaten the sovereign's position as the symbol of Britain. And worse still, he *acted* like a ruler, treating the Queen, however solemnly and respectfully, as a figurehead, refusing to divulge to her the individual opinions of members of his Cabinet and making it odiously clear that only her signature, not her opinion, was required. Last but not least, he scorned her pleasure in imperial pomp and power. He made her feel, in short, like a silly girl.

Mary Ponsonby, as early as 1878, foresaw the explosion that would occur if the Queen should be subjected to being hauled out of the warm and fragrant bath of Disraeli's premiership and plunged again into the icy waters of Gladstone's. She wrote to her husband:

I *do* think Dizzy has worked the idea of personal government to its logical conclusion, and the seed was sown by Stockmar and the Prince. While they lived, the current of public opinion, especially among the Ministers, kept the thing between bounds, but they established the superstition in the Queen's mind about her own prerogative, and we who know her, know also perfectly how that superstition, devoid as it is of even a shadow of real political value, can be worked by an unscrupulous Minister to his advantage and the country's ruin. If there comes a real collision between the Queen and the House of Commons (say, for instance, that the country insists on Gladstone for the next Liberal Prime Minister) it is quite possible she would turn restive, *dorlotède* as she has been by Dizzy's high-sounding platitudes, and then her reign will end in a fiasco *or* she prepares one for the Prince of Wales; for I do think in a tussle of that sort, and I do hope and pray it should be so, that the People win the day.

Imagine what the Queen would have said to the last sentence!

Two years later, in 1880, the Conservatives lost a general election, and Disraeli resigned as Prime Minister, without waiting for Parliament to meet. Lord Hartington was the Liberal leader in the House of Commons, Lord Granville in the Lords; either would have been an appropriate choice for the Queen to have made, but it was obvious that nobody could form a government without Gladstone, who was responsible for the great Liberal victory at the polls. The Queen was at Baden-Baden, far from the scene, and, as many had foreseen, violently embittered by the defeat of her favourite. Ponsonby shared his wife's fears of unconstitutional behaviour. He tried to believe that the Queen was 'determined to carry out the Constitutional principles most conscientiously', but he could not predict what she might do when 'preyed upon by other influences'. He wrote to Mary:

The change from this [Disraeli's premiership] to Gladstone would be most trying to her and in fact she says she will not have him. What this fully means one cannot say but she has declared she would abdicate rather than submit to dictation. Gladstone once told me that this threat of abdication was the greatest power the Sovereign possessed – nothing could stand against it, for the position of a Minister who forced it on would be untenable. True. But on the other hand what a terrible victory it would be for her. It would be almost ruin. And I earnestly hope that these mutterings may not go beyond me. I am really very sorry for the Queen for it is a most painful and trying moment. If she takes either Granville or Hartington she will believe and not without reason that they will be influenced by Gladstone so that unless he is made a friend of I foresee a time of trouble and anxiety.

He now submitted the strongest of all his memoranda to the Queen:

Lt.-General Sir Henry Ponsonby presents his humble duty to Your Majesty.

In reply to Your Majesty's enquiry he believes that the Liberal leaders find it nearly impossible to form a Government unless it is publicly known that Mr Gladstone declines office. And that if Your Majesty sends for either Lord Granville or Lord Hartington they will be obliged to ask leave to consult him.

Sir Henry Ponsonby looks forward with some anxiety to the future. He must confess he would prefer to see Mr Gladstone in the Cabinet rather than out of it. In the Cabinet he would be invested with responsibility, advised by his colleagues and influenced by Your Majesty. He is loyal and devoted to the Queen who can control him. He would be a strong barrier against the movements of factious men and can and will keep the Liberal party in order.

Disraeli, consulted by the Queen, advised her to send for Lord Hartington, which she did. While he and Lord Granville were in conference with her, Ponsonby, knowing that they were going to insist that she call Gladstone, was on tenterhooks. When he went to their room after the audience was over, Granville 'kissed his hand with a smile like a ballet girl receiving applause', and Hartington 'threw himself into a chair with "Ha! Ha!"' There had been no difficulty. All had been smooth.

Had there ever been a real danger? Was Ponsonby's tact really necessary to keep the Queen on her throne? Probably not. Victoria had a basic sense of just how far people could be pushed. I very much doubt that she would ever have acted so extremely as to precipitate a general Cabinet resignation. It is even possible that she consciously used poor Sir Henry as her sounding-board, testing out on him all the expletives that tact might require her to suppress or at least to modify in direct correspondence with her ministers. If with Disraeli she was playing Mary Stuart, perhaps with Ponsonby she was playing Elizabeth.

It is further evidence of her realism that she knew, whenever she decided to be really naughty, that she would have to do so behind the private secretary's back. Towards the end of Gladstone's second ministry, when he was planning to withdraw from the Sudan, she wrote directly to Lady Wolseley, wife of the Commander-in-Chief in Egypt: 'In *strict confidence* I *must* tell you I think the Government are *more incorrigible* than ever, and I do think your husband should use *strong* language to them, and

OVERLEAF The Queen's Garden Party at Windsor Castle. Victoria receives her guests on the lawn.

even threaten to resign, if he does not receive strong support and liberty of action ... But it *must never appear*, or Lord Wolseley *ever let out*, the hint I give you!' Even this was not enough for her. She had to write to Lord Wolseley himself to beg him 'to *resist* and strongly oppose *all* idea of retreat' and to *destroy* her letter! Certainly this is not the stern Tudor voice that warned Robert Cecil: 'Little man, little man, the word "must" is never used to princes!' It is a scheming Victoria, a nervous Victoria, trying to get around her stubborn Prime Minister. It is a woman who has learned her Constitution and *knows* that she is operating outside it. What would Stockmar have said to such a subterfuge? One veils one's eyes.

But the important thing, in the last analysis, is that the Queen *had* learned. In 1885 she was angry that Gladstone's government was doing what she deemed the wrong thing; she was not questioning their constitutional right to do it. She was acting improperly, yes, but in a long reign no monarch can be constitutional *all* the time. The dangerous time for Victoria was not so much when she tried secretly to frustrate Gladstone's African policy as when she considered refusing to ask him to form a government.

What should always be remembered about Ponsonby and the Queen is that it was she who appointed him to his post and she who kept him there for twenty-five years despite his Whig inclinations and his unconcealed admiration for Gladstone. The Queen also liked and admired his Liberal wife and appointed his son Frederick to be her equerry. These are certainly grounds for inferring that she had some insight into her own need for a check on her temper. Ponsonby may have represented her opportunity to count to a hundred, a built-in brake or alarm signal. If this was so, the Queen herself deserves much of the credit for him.

The last decade of Victoria's reign was the finest; her long slow sunset gave out a splendid glow. Sir Henry died in 1895, six years before the end of the reign, but his job was done. He was less needed now. The royal temper had become milder, the royal humour more benign; the Queen appeared constantly before her adoring public. Political issues concerned her less; Lord Salisbury possessed all her confidence. Her position in the world was too exalted to allow of fretting about parliamentary squabbles; her empire was greater than Rome's; Kaiser and Czar called her 'grandmamma'. No human being in history has achieved such eminence. She was beyond the Constitution; she had her own special niche in the universe; she was, to everyone, 'the Queen'.

A photograph of Sir Henry Ponsonby in later life. His tactful management of the Queen and her affairs was appreciated by all.

Sir Henry had been only one of the many props that she could now discard. She stood alone.

But we should end a piece on Sir Henry with a tribute to him from the greatest statesman of the age. When Gladstone retired in 1894, a year before Sir Henry's death, he received no word of thanks or praise from his sovereign. He did receive, however, a graceful letter from the private secretary who had undoubtedly done his best in vain to persuade the Queen to some more generous action. Gladstone acknowledged his letter with the following: 'I have known and have liked and admired all the men who have served the Queen in your delicate and responsible office ... But forgive me for saying you are "to the manner born" and such a combination of tact and temper with loyalty, intelligence and truth I cannot expect to see again.'

Chapter Five

WILLIAM EWART GLADSTONE

Shortly after the death of William E. Gladstone in 1898, in his ninetieth year, a little volume of 'Talks' with the deceased statesman was brought out by the Hon. Lionel A. Tollemache. The author was a pygmy would-be Boswell who tried to make up for the paucity of his material by filling in the blank spaces with his own opinions. He did not succeed in cornering his subject until he caught the old man on a winter excursion to Biarritz, but then he attached himself to his prey with some of the tenacity of his Scottish model. Occasionally he incurred the rumbling wrath of his victim, as Boswell so often did with Dr Johnson. This happened when he asked Gladstone to reconcile what he deemed two conflicting biblical texts, one supporting the Greek view of immortality, which represents the soul as surviving without the body, and the other seeming to back the Christian theory of bodily resurrection, which does not assign to the soul an independent existence. Perhaps it was too much for a tea party: 'I fear that I cannot have made my reasoning plain to Mr Gladstone; for he answered with unusual heat, "I really cannot answer such questions. The Almighty never took me into His confidence as to why there is to be a Day of Judgment." I felt it was impossible to press the matter further.' One is reminded of Father William's rebuke in *Alice in Wonderland*: 'Be off, or I'll kick you downstairs!'

For the most part, however, Tollemache's relations with the benign old parliamentarian seem to have been serene. One follows them with a kind of fascination, the officious bubbling questioner and the solemn, kindly, sometimes impatient seer, through the wide corridors of a gilded Gallic seaside hotel, attending to their discourse on themes as far removed from their locale as: the existence of Hell, the moral weakness of Thomas Cranmer, the materialism of Americans, the debt of the Greeks to the Jews, the genius of Napoleon, the public's failure to appreciate British poetesses, Horace's comparison of Diana with Proserpine, flogging at Eton and which era of history one would have preferred to have lived in. Gladstone, of course, chose the Homeric. Had

PREVIOUS PAGE The young William Gladstone at the time of his marriage.

122

he not already proved, in three large volumes, that Homer shared with the Hebrew prophets a divine inspiration? Mr Gladstone's favourite epoch had to be purged of paganism.

It is remarkable that the man who dominated British politics for so many decades, who was four times prime minister, who mastered every figure of the Exchequer, who swayed multitudes with his impassioned oratory, who forged together and then broke apart the Liberal Party, the 'grand old man' of the people whose picture hung on thousands of humble kitchen walls, should have been able to turn, with an equal interest, from the question of vaccination to the character of Achilles. One is reminded of the wide range of subjects in the lifelong correspondence between Justice Oliver Wendell Holmes and Sir Frederick Pollock, but neither of those great lawyer scholars was engaged in the harassing fray of party politics.

One is not, however, reminded of their literary tastes. Gladstone considered Scott the greatest of novelists, and he became 'half-angry' with a young lady who insisted that she derived more pleasure from Thackeray and George Eliot. Asked what modern novels he admired, he mentioned Baring Gould's *Mahalah*. He could not finish *Diana of the Crossways*; he deemed *Le Misanthrope* and *Tartuffe* third-rate plays, and he quoted with approval Tennyson's opinion of Whitman: that as he could not sing he should write in prose. One feels that morals, *his* morals, played the major role in his aesthetic judgments: 'He was asked if he had observed the singular absence of the sense of sin in the works of American divines of all schools. "Ah," said he slowly, "the sense of sin – that is the great want in modern life; it is wanting in our sermons, wanting everywhere!" This was said slowly and reflectively, almost like a monologue.'

If Gladstone's intellect was like a mighty river, his morality was like a torrential rain. It flooded the river and caused it to jump its banks and overflow the countryside, obliterating boundaries. Lord Palmerston said that he was a dangerous man because he could convince himself of anything. He was like an Old Testament prophet; when he heard Jehovah's bidding, he would act, and it did not make the slightest difference whether what he did today was inconsistent with what he had done yesterday. Like Merlin, he followed his gleam. It is small wonder that his opposition should have been divided into those who regarded him as a religious fanatic and those who dubbed him a wily and opportunistic hypocrite. He simply did not behave like other people. There was no fence of common sense or decorum to hem him in, and he might end up establishing Homer as a Christian, or disestablishing a Church that he had pledged himself to support, or roaming the streets of London to seek out and redeem prostitutes, without caring in the least how he might look to others. He not only could convince himself that God was behind him; he expected others to recognize the divinity of his push. If he was much loved, he was also much hated.

This sense of divine mission, which set him so far apart from other contemporary statesmen, was a tremendous force. Those who maintained that it was simple megalomania used to point out that he often acted, and very astutely, in his own best interests. But just as often he did not. He published books on Church matters with extreme conclusions which made him seem ridiculous. He went off to the Ionian Islands on a diplomatic *cul de sac* of a mission that no astute politician would have dreamed of accepting. He resigned the leadership of the Liberal Party in Disraeli's second ministry, with the result that the Queen was not constitutionally bound to call on him after his great electoral victory in 1880. He risked his reputation to save prostitutes. And finally he wrecked his last two ministries and his party by pushing home rule for Ireland. The really extraordinary thing about his career is that he triumphed in spite of himself.

To this observer he begins to stand out, after a long blurring, as the greatest man of his epoch. He seems, to us now, very much what his contemporary admirers believed him to be. Perhaps God *was* on his side. Consider his positions on the great issues of the day. He favoured universal male suffrage and a strict subordination of the Crown and the House of Lords to the Commons. He believed that the Empire should be diminished rather than expanded and in self-rule for Ireland. Who would dispute these positions today? Only in his *laissez faire* philosophy of economics does he seem out-of-date to modern eyes, and this he shared with almost all politicians of his time. Not even the Radicals, like Bright and Cobden, favoured the welfare state.

There is one great consistency in Gladstone's long career: he always tried to act as he believed God – a God who loved all men – would want him to act. It was this that made him bigger than his contemporaries and that made his decisions so often the right ones. What his political life seems to suggest is that honesty and a deep concern for all mankind, in domestic as well as in international politics, may, just possibly, in the long run, pay off.

Hawarden Castle, Gladstone's beloved retreat in the country.

Catherine Gladstone
from a painting by
F. R. Say. Catherine was
something of a husband-
worshipper.

He was born with all the advantages that Disraeli lacked. He was handsome – in a very British manner – and rich. His father had come from Scotland to Liverpool, where he had risen to be a leading corn merchant, a baronet and a member of Parliament. Even more importantly for Gladstone, this parent had always considered it his particular mission in life to sponsor and further the political career of his brilliant son. William had only to pass with every honour through Eton and Oxford and then take a seat in the House of Commons. He married young and happily, although Catherine, a husband-worshipper, sometimes embarrassed him by her violent epistolary appeals to colleagues who in her opinion had failed properly to back him up, but in this he suffered no more than Disraeli or Rosebery. Tactlessness seems to have been a feature of Victorian political wives. Gladstone, at any rate, before the age of thirty, was a rising man, with a reputation in Parliament, a large town house at Carleton Terrace and a castle in the country. It would have ruined an American youth.

But nothing was ever going to be easy for Gladstone. The more obstacles that his father cleared away for him, the more he piled up for himself. For he had been born with a violent nature and the most formidable conscience of his age. As his wife told his biographer, John Morley, her husband had two sides: one impetuous, impatient, irrestrainable, the other all self-control, able to dismiss everything but the great central aim. He had achieved self-mastery 'by the natural power of his character and by incessant wrestling in prayer'. Gladstone had had the greatest difficulty choosing his career between the ministry and politics, and he would not even allow Catherine to hire a cook until he had first exhaustively discussed the candidate's religious principles.

He seems funny to us, and he seemed funny to the generation that preceded his own, but he did not seem funny to millions of his contemporaries. An age of gravity was dawning. The great aristocrats who had taken leisurely turns at their self-imposed task of governing Britain, the charming, easy-going cynical Lord Melbourne, the emphatic, mocking, bluffing Lord Palmerston, to whom no subject, not even their own pre-eminence, was sacred, would have to share their power now with middle-class millionaires who did not hesitate to bring God into the dining-room, even with the port. The deity was to be Gladstone's partner in the task of redeeming England for six decades.

He began his political life as a Tory, representing what was virtually a pocket borough of the Duke of Newcastle. From this Conservative start, he moved steadily to the left through a long lifetime. There was considerable room. The young Gladstone had believed in limiting the franchise to voters of substantial property; he was a strict Anglican who insisted that the government should never give a penny, even indirectly, to any but the established Church, and in the battle against slavery (influenced perhaps by a father who owned blacks in the colonies) he advocated only a gradual emancipation, geared to an education programme. But his conscience was not going to allow him to remain fixed in any of these positions, or, indeed, in any position with which he might afterwards replace them. Life was going to be an endless task of self-examination and reappraisal, and promotion would always sound a bell to warn him that it might be temptation in disguise.

Cardinal Henry Manning, one of Gladstone's closest friends, to whom he often turned for advice.

In 1843, at the age of thirty-four, Gladstone was invited to join Sir Robert Peel's Cabinet as President of the Board of Trade. Even in that day of early political successes, it was unusual to reach Cabinet level so young, and if Gladstone had had the ambition that his detractors ascribe to him, he would have accepted with alacrity. Yet what did he do? He raised the question with Sir Robert as to whether he were not already too far committed against the Government's position with respect to the union of two bishoprics in North Wales to accept. These bishoprics, Bangor and St Asaph, had been united by Parliament in 1836, but there was still some public feeling in favour of their severance, and Gladstone had strong feelings on the subject. He consulted with his two great friends, James Hope and Henry Manning (neither of whom had yet become a Catholic), and they advised him that the issue was too narrow to support a refusal to serve. Later on, Gladstone wrote that their decision had been the correct one and that they had been not his 'tempters' but, on the contrary, his 'good angels'.

Sir Robert may have had a premonition then that this very serious young man was going to be a difficult crew-member to hold on to. Gladstone's scrupulousness seems almost like self-destruction in the light of modern psychiatry, but worse was to come. Only a year later he resigned from the government because of the proposed extension by Parliament of the public endowment for a seminary for the training of Roman Catholic clergy at Maynooth, in Ireland.

His position over the Maynooth Bill confused his

contemporaries and seems impossibly quixotic to modern eyes. The original endowment had been voted by the Irish Parliament, Protestant though it was, and accepted after 1800 even by anti-Catholic political leaders as an inherited statute resulting from the union of the two legislatures. Macaulay has pointed out how stingily the British had behaved towards a Church they had plundered: they had taken over the magnificently endowed colleges of Oxford and Cambridge and given the Roman Catholics a Dotheboys Hall in return. Gladstone was even persuaded of this, but he nonetheless felt that the Maynooth Bill was inconsistent with his earlier stand on the sacred and exclusive obligation of the State towards its own established Church. Would not serving under a government that carried out the provisions of the Maynooth Bill make him seem untrustworthy? The scruple seems finely strained, but even more so in view of the fact that Gladstone, after his resignation from the government, proceeded to support and vote for the bill! He admitted that his behaviour might cause him to be regarded 'as fastidious and fanciful, fitter for a dreamer or possibly a schoolman than for the active purposes of public life in a busy and moving age'. Indeed it did. Disraeli told people that Gladstone's career was over.

Ironically enough, it was Disraeli himself who offered the occasion for its resuscitation, seven years later, when, as Chancellor of the Exchequer under Lord Derby, he submitted a budget that Gladstone was able to tear to pieces. Gladstone, as Lord Aberdeen observed, was 'terrible on the rebound'. He had disliked Disraeli from the beginning; it is obvious how the latter's jaded cynicism must have galled the serious man of God. Without this dislike Gladstone might even for a time have joined forces with the Protectionist party. As it was, Disraeli provided an additional impetus to his move to liberalism.

Certainly, the contrast in their personalities has provided the most popular drama in Victorian politics. Disraeli's budget made Gladstone, according to one report, actually 'foam at the mouth'. In much the same way, Disraeli's indifference to the Bulgarian atrocities was to make Gladstone explode from his retirement a quarter of a century later. If Gladstone's actions were determined by what he deemed an impulse from the Almighty, perhaps they could be quickened as well by an apprehension of the spirit of evil. He did not admit formally to a belief in Hell or the devil, but if he had, it is easy to surmise whose shape Mephistopheles would have taken.

OPPOSITE A cartoon of Gladstone by Spy from *Vanity Fair*.

OVERLEAF A painting of Balmoral Castle by August Becker, executed in 1865. Victoria and Albert decided to buy Balmoral in 1844, following a royal visit to Scotland. As it was originally a small castle, the Queen decided to rebuild it, and this was completed in 1853.

Gladstone not only tore up Disraeli's budget; he brought down Derby's government, and it was inevitable that Lord Aberdeen, the new premier, should offer him the Exchequer. Gladstone was to achieve a success with the chancellorship, which he held from 1852 to 1855 and again from 1859 to 1866, less qualified than that which he was to achieve with the premiership. He found that he could dominate figures as even he could never dominate men. Morley has rightly said that there is nothing more deadly than the resuscitation of dead budgets, so the following passage from his great biography must suffice to convey an impression of Gladstone's financial legerdemain:

Enthusiastic journalists with the gift of a poetic pen told their millions of readers how, after weeks of malign prophecy, the great trickster in Downing Street would be proved to have beggared the Exchequer, that years of gloom and insolvency awaited us, suddenly, the moment the magician chose to draw aside the veil, the darkness rolled away; he had fluttered out of sight the whole race of sombre Volscians, and where the gazers dreaded to see a gulf they beheld a golden monument of glorious finance.

Gladstone was uneasy at being in the Aberdeen government at the outbreak of the Crimean War, and he studied the dispatches carefully to determine if there existed a moral issue of sufficient depth to justify the shedding of blood. He decided at length that perhaps there did, that perhaps such an issue had been created by Russian aggression, but he was quickly satisfied after a few engagements that Moscow had been adequately punished, and following the fall of the Aberdeen government for its inefficiency in military matters, he enthusiastically took up the unpopular cause of early peace.

At fifty, the age he had now achieved, Gladstone seemed determined to be a failure. He was still carrying on an almost public debate with himself as to his true party alignment. He had rejected Disraeli's offer of the leadership of the old Protectionist party. He had taken himself out of the political fray by accepting a thankless mission to investigate the legal status and future of the Ionian Islands, a discontented British protectorate. He had voted in favour of the Derby government on an issue of confidence and thereafter joined its successor as Chancellor of the Exchequer. He had taken the unpopular side in pressing peace with Russia, in opposing the panic on papal aggression and on the bill of divorce. No wonder Greville described him then as the 'half-dead, broken-down and tempest-tossed Gladstone'.

OPPOSITE A decorative plate published to celebrate the Jubilee of 1897, depicting the Queen's homes – Windsor Castle, Balmoral and Osborne – and members of her family.

PUNCH, OR THE LONDON CHARIVARI.—June 19, 1880.

LABOUR AND REST.

Ex-Head Gardener (*retired from business*). "WELL, WILLIAM, YER DON'T SEEM TO BE MAKIN' MUCH PROGRESS—*DO* YER!"
New Head Gardener. "WHY NO, BENJAMIN; YOU LEFT THE PLACE IN SUCH A PRECIOUS MESS!!"

The enmity between Gladstone and Disraeli was the subject of much ribald commentary in the press.

There was one issue, however, in which he triumphed and which seems, looking back over his long career, to mark the dividing point between Gladstone, the liberal conservative, and Gladstone, the conservative liberal. This was the tax on paper, which tended to limit the printing of cheap newspapers for the poor. Gladstone proposed its abolition in his budget, but the House of Lords passed it. Determined to bring the Lords into line, Gladstone, in the next year's budget, reinstated the elimination of the paper duties and insisted that the Lords either accept the budget as a whole or throw it out altogether. He carried his point, which marked the end of the practice by the upper chamber of the piecemeal cutting-up of budgets. It was also the beginning of a battle between the two chambers which lasted for the rest of Gladstone's political life. The Lords had the last word when they threw out his second Home Rule Bill in 1894, but they wrote their own doom in doing so, and before the First World War their powers had been largely eliminated. Gladstone had now emerged as 'the people's William', in time to become the Grand Old Man.

Philip Magnus, whose excellent life of Gladstone supplements Morley's massive biography in much the same way as Robert Blake's life of Disraeli does the longer work by Buckle and Monypenny, demonstrates that whenever Gladstone was personally exposed to scenes of human injustice and intolerance he would be outraged, but that without such personal exposure he was inclined to accept the status quo. Where, however, Gladstone differed from his fellow men was that his outrage, once aroused, was never appeased, and so his moral outlook steadily expanded through a long life until he was liberal in every great public issue. Thus, his position changed from a staggered to a total emancipation of slaves, from a limited franchise to a vote for every British male, and from a narrow Anglicanism to a toleration of all religions.

Once converted to a cause, he remained so to the end. In 1851, on a visit to the kingdom of Naples, he attended the trial of Poerio and listened for hours to the obviously perjured testimony of government witnesses. He visited the defendant in jail and saw with his own eyes political prisoners chained two and two in double irons with common felons. He branded the old regime of the Bourbons as 'the negation of God erected into a system of government', and he came home to espouse passionately the cause of freedom in Italy.

In the same year he unsuccessfully opposed a bill prohibiting the establishment by the Pope of geographical bishoprics in Britain. He made one of his greatest speeches, ending on this ringing note:

You speak of the progress of the Roman Catholic religion, and you pretend to meet that progress by a measure false in principle as it is ludicrous in extent. You must meet the progress of that spiritual system by the progress of another; you can never do it by penal enactment. Here, once for all, I enter my most solemn, deliberate and earnest protest against all attempt to meet the spiritual dangers of our Church by temporal legislation of a penal character.

More and more intensely now, he began to see his life's mission as a religious one. It was to dedicate himself to the task of teaching men and nations to govern themselves by schooling their passions and so to realize on earth the spirit of the Christian ethic.

On the eve of his fifty-ninth birthday he recorded in his diary: 'The Almighty seems to sustain me and spare me for some purpose of his own, deeply unworthy as I know myself to be.'

He was not, of course, a liberal in the modern sense. Indeed, by our standards he was an economic Tory. In an interesting little book entitled *Mr Gladstone at Oxford*, C. R. L. Fletcher describes the great man's visit as a guest of All Soul's College for a week in the winter of 1890. He amazed his audience at dinner by telling them that the Duke of Wellington had been quite right in defending the control that the old House of Lords had exercised over the Commons by means of the pocket boroughs, claiming that this had established an ideal as well as a real equilibrium between the component parts of Parliament. He then went on to say that the Reform Bill of 1832 had destroyed this equilibrium and that thereafter the Constitution was logically bound to develop on purely democratic or socialist lines, a result which he appeared to regard as a doubtful blessing. This sounds like Stockmar himself. And, finally, he observed that in point of ability and efficiency, Britain had never been better governed than in the period preceding the first Reform Bill!

Basically, what Gladstone believed was that free and unhampered individuals, rather than government, would ultimately relieve social and economic distress. When accused in a dialogue with Ruskin of being a 'leveller', he stoutly denied it, insisting, on the contrary, that he was an 'inequalitarian' who believed in aristocracy, or the rule of the best. But he counted on freedom to bring that best to power.

Was he practical? Without strenuous legislative control could the social and economic injustices of Victorian life have ever been adjusted? Without the huge military budgets that he so deplored could Germany have been defeated in two world wars? All one can say is that Gladstone, who was always changing, would presumably have changed with the times. He would probably have been closer to the Labour Party than to the Conservatives in the period between the wars, and I feel sure that the evil of Hitler would have placed him squarely behind Winston Churchill. What I conclude is simply that his conscientious search for the moral question in every issue was of an ultimate practical benefit to the British in his lifetime.

Consider the great issues on which he was so bitterly resisted. How many today would think it fair for Ireland to pay for an established Protestant Church? How many would insist on a property qualification for a ballot? How many would oppose an oath by affirmation? How many, assuming Ireland to be still a part of the United Kingdom, would oppose Home Rule? How many would favour the extension of the Empire and the exploitation of natives?

Even in the area of economics there is room at least to admire Gladstone's passionate faith in the individual. Whatever reservations one may have about it, it certainly points in the opposite direction from that taken by most of the world today. Gladstone would have hated Communism as he hated Disraeli.

Success came early for Gladstone, but the highest honours were delayed. He did not become the leader of the Liberal Party in the House of Commons until 1865, and he had to wait until 1868 before replacing Disraeli as prime minister. It must have been bitter tea for him that the Reform Bill of 1867, the essence of which he had long advocated, should have been carried to its final passage by the Conservatives. Disraeli, who, only a year before, had prophesied that the end of the seven-pound franchise would mean a House of Commons consisting of 'a horde of selfish and obscure mediocrities, incapable of anything but mischief, and that mischief devised and regulated by the raging demagogue of the hour', took all the credit for the new democracy by his rapid change of face. It might have confirmed his opponent in any suspicion of satanic trickery. Who remembered in Disraeli's triumph, when *Punch* depicted him as an oriental despot with a whip driving the Commons, including his principal opponent, into the Temple of Reform, that it was Gladstone who three years before had shocked people with the statement: 'I venture to say that every man who is not presumably incapacitated by some consideration of personal unfitness or of political danger, is morally entitled to come within the pale of the Constitution'?

Disraeli's triumph, however, was a short one. The ministry that he led, after Derby's resignation, endured for less than a year. When word was brought to Gladstone, after the Liberal victory at the polls, that the Queen had sent for him to form a government, he was engaged in felling a tree at Hawarden. Morley describes the scene with reverence. 'Gladstone paused and then uttered these words with deep earnestness and great intensity: "My mission is to pacify Ireland." He then in silence resumed his work with the axe until the tree was down.'

Felling trees at Hawarden was Gladstone's favourite hobby, and one he was engaged in doing when word came that the Queen had sent for him to form a government.

It would be unfair to deprive the reader of Lord Randolph Churchill's quite different appreciation of Gladstone's favourite manual exercise. Here is how Churchill visualizes the visit of a group of working men to Hawarden to view the great statesman so engaged:

For the purposes of recreation he has selected the felling of trees, and we may usefully remark that his amusements, like his politics, are constantly destructive. The forest laments in order that Mr Gladstone may perspire ... The working men were guided through the ornamental grounds into the wide-spreading park, strewn with the wreckage and the ruins of the Prime Minister's sport. All around them, we may suppose, lay the rotting trunks of once umbrageous trees; all around them, tossed by the winds, were boughs and bark and withered shoots ... They come suddenly on the Prime Minister and Master Herbert in scanty attire and profuse perspiration, engaged in the destruction of a gigantic oak, just giving its dying groan. They are permitted to gaze and worship and adore, and having conducted themselves with exemplary propriety, are each of them presented with a few chips as a memorial of that memorable scene.

When Gladstone left his tree-cutting to take up the reins of government, he was true to his word about his mission. He went right to work in the teeth of the sovereign, the lords and the bishops to disestablish the Church of Ireland. He also introduced an Irish Land Act which opened up the movement for agrarian reform. English law had never recognized the rights given by ancient custom to the Irish tenant farmers. In England the tenant had no rights other than those spelled out in his lease, but in Ireland the relationship between landlord and tenant with respect to farmed land had been more of a partnership. This had been originally a simple misunderstanding on the part of the English, but it was a misunderstanding that had been encouraged by the landlords.

Another accomplishment of Gladstone's first ministry was the abolition of the sale of military commissions. This, unfortunately, brought him into collision with the Queen, who was very jealous of all her prerogatives, especially in the military area. From this period may be dated the strong dislike on her part which was to last until Gladstone's death.

At the beginning of any discussion of this famous antagonism, we should bear in mind the warning of Frank Hardie in his excellent *The Political Influence of Queen Victoria* that politics played just as large a role as personalities in Queen Victoria's dislikes. Although she started her reign as a Whig, or Liberal, under the influence of Lord Melbourne, she was soon converted to the Conservative persuasion by Sir Robert Peel and remained a hardened Tory for the rest of her life. One need not take too seriously her frequent boasts that in 'true liberalism' she would bow to none. The fact is that she believed in a strong sovereign, a strong upper house, a strong military and no income or death taxes. She distrusted the lower orders, whom she thought of as a potential mob, and she opposed the extension of the franchise to all men and to any women. Once she had clearly taken in the fact that Gladstone was a 'radical' – and by her definition he certainly was one – there could be no further question of her liking him. Disraeli, committed to Gladstone's principles, would have found all his arts of flattery vain.

Lord Rosebery is evidence of this. He had a great head start in the Queen's favour: he was young, handsome, charming and the son of one of her bridesmaids. He treated her with all of Disraeli's deference and none of his oiliness. It is small wonder that he should have pleased her, for his respect and awe of her were genuine. But nothing could bring her round to the smallest support of his liberal policies. It is true that she never came to dislike him – he was too inherently likeable – but she gave him a very

Lord Rosebery was young and handsome and treated Victoria with deference, but she would not agree with any of his liberal policies.

hard time, and he always told his friends afterwards that his brief ministry had been, for this reason, a shattering experience.

It seems a pity that the large common denominator of Victorianism that existed between the Queen and Gladstone should not have softened their relationship, but it did not. Perhaps they were confronted with a simple failure in communication. Certainly Gladstone would have been sympathetic had he, rather than Archbishop Benson, received this confidence from his sovereign: 'As I get older I cannot understand the world. I cannot comprehend its littleness. When I look at the frivolities and bitternesses, it seems to me as if they were all a little mad.' Does not that sound more Gladstone's affair than Disraeli's? Had the Prince Consort lived, things might have been better. He liked and respected Gladstone, and the latter admired the Prince's conscientiousness and industry, although he had been shocked when Albert had told him that he was happy about the new papal doctrine of the immaculate conception because it would tend to 'expose and explode' the Roman Church. Gladstone had respectfully remonstrated that all men must have an interest in the well-being of the Christian community, but 'no assent, even qualified'

Victoria's dislike of Gladstone became almost paranoic after his first ministry and lasted to his death.

to this was obtainable from the Prince. Still, two men who could be so serious about a papal decree were bound at least sometimes to be mutually sympathetic. The Queen, on the other hand, did not care to be lectured to about Church history.

Gladstone, as is often pointed out, treated her too much as a sovereign, too little as a woman. He was too candid, too detailed, too serious. He did not sugar coat his pills; he would have thought to do so a kind of *lèse majesté*. But the Queen had no use for that kind of respect. She saw him as a threat to the monarchy, the Church and the aristocracy. What she did not see was that only a sovereign as Gladstone defined one would be able to survive in the future Britain. Victoria's successors accepted easily and wisely what was wormwood to her. Her great-great-granddaughter, Elizabeth II, would have been Gladstone's ideal of a queen.

What I find hardest to forgive is the Queen's treatment of Gladstone on his final retirement in 1894, at the age of eighty-five, because of deafness and failing sight. No matter what her opinion of his policies, no matter how low she may have rated his contribution to British public life, she should have shown some appreciation of that great lifetime of toil devoted sincerely (as even she believed) to what he deemed his country's good. Never did she show herself smaller than in her frigid acceptance of his demission, so unlike her usual kindness and courtesy:

Though the Queen has already accepted Mr Gladstone's resignation, and has taken leave of him, she does not like to leave his letter tendering his resignation unanswered. She therefore writes these few lines to say that she thinks, after so many years of arduous labour and responsibility, he is right in wishing to be relieved at his age of these arduous duties, and she trusts he will be able to enjoy peace and quiet, with his excellent and devoted wife, in health and happiness, and that his eyesight may improve.

The Queen would gladly have conferred a Peerage on Mr Gladstone, but she knows that he would not accept it.

Not a syllable of praise, not a word of thanks! It was from the ever courteous Ponsonby that Gladstone received his only tribute in the Court. Small wonder that he exploded with uncharacteristic bitterness. Philip Magnus describes his reaction:

A few days later, in a private memorandum, he wrote:

'Granted that the absence of any act and word of regard, regret, or interest, is absolutely deserved. But then I have a wife. Of her, HM, in her concluding letter wrote in terms (which conveyed some implication of reproach to me) of warm interest and praise.' He thought that the Queen might have presented her portrait to Mrs Gladstone or 'some voluntary offering ... But there was nothing of the kind. For I cannot reckon as anything what appeared to be a twopenny-half-penny scrap, photographic or other, sent during the forenoon of our departure by the hand of a footman.'

At the end of his first ministry in 1874, Gladstone, at sixty-five, was disgusted to see the despised rival take office again with a large Conservative majority and the prospect of indefinite rule.

Feeling that his political life was now really over, he gave up the leadership of his party in the House of Commons, although keeping his seat, and retired to his beloved Hawarden where he hoped to devote his remaining years to literature and Church studies.

In the 1880s he was to build a fireproof wing to the castle, called the octagon room, to house his vast correspondence. On its shelves are stacked more than a hundred thousand letters – from royalties, politicians, clerics, philosophers, writers, artists and simple constituents. The range of subjects is seemingly infinite, as was the range of Gladstone's reading and thought. He was one of the last of the great literary statesmen, a breed which the modern stress of political elections does not seem to grow.

Homer and Dante were lifelong passions – Homer, the more intense. Gladstone wrote a text to prove that the inspiration of the Greek poet was akin to the inspiration of the Hebrews, that the Odyssey and the Iliad were just as integral parts of the prelude

William and Catherine Gladstone with the Prince and Princess of Wales. Gladstone and Edward had a sympathetic understanding of each other's difficult relationship with Victoria.

to Christianity as the Old Testament. The great Jowett termed this treatise 'nonsense', but from a religious point of view it makes considerable sense. Gladstone wanted to embrace all history in the fold of Christianity; he could not bear to have the ancients left out, any more than unbaptized infants and heretics. He would not have relished Heaven while there languished a single soul in Hell. Why should a great poet, and a man of great heart, like Homer, not be as much a herald of Christ as John the Baptist? There may be more than a touch of naïveté in Gladstone's religious writings, but the sentiment is always Christian in the very finest sense. His idea of the true Church was that it should be generous. He could not believe, he wrote, 'that God's tender mercies are restricted to a small portion of the human family'.

In literature he always showed greater taste and feeling for the classic authors than for those of his own time, probably because, in the case of the former, he felt less obliged to make moral judgments. He could give himself to Horace's Odes, for example, with a detachment and an enthusiasm that he could not afford to give to Swinburne's ballads, although he enjoyed the latter. Here is a translation of the Ode to Pyrrha which catches some of the tight wording and compacted thought of the original:

> What scented stripling, Pyrrha, woos thee now,
>   In pleasant grotto, all with roses fair?
> For whom those auburn tresses bindest thou
>   With simple care?
>
> Full oft shall he thine altered faith bewail,
>   His altered gods: and his unwonted gaze
> Shall watch the waters darkening to the gale
>   In wild amaze:
>
> Who now believing gloats on golden charms;
>   Who hopes thee ever void, and ever kind;
> Nor knows they changeful heart, nor the alarms
>   Of changeful wind.
>
> For me, let Neptune's temple-wall declare
>   How, safe-escaped, in votive offering,
> My dripping garments own, suspended there,
>   Him Ocean-King.

In 1876 the revolt of the Christian provinces of Turkey in Bosnia

144

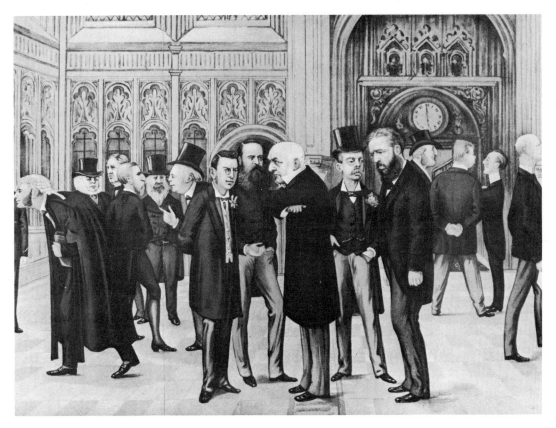

and Herzegovina was suppressed with a hideous cruelty which brought the old statesman of Hawarden out of his semi-retirement with a roar of righteous wrath. Disraeli's cynical suggestion that the Press reports of torture were probably exaggerated because the Turks had 'more expeditious methods' of dealing with their opponents, was all that was needed to bring his old rival's fury to a white heat. In a pamphlet which had a huge sale, he branded the Turks as 'the one great anti-human specimen of humanity' and charged them with the basest and blackest outrages within the memory of man. There was not a criminal in Europe, Gladstone cried, nor a cannibal in the South Seas, who would not rise to protest 'the floodgates of lust' and 'the dire refinements of cruelty'.

He took his campaign to the House of Commons, where Disraeli's government was arguing that Britain's interest was to bolster Turkey against Russia: 'You talk to me of the established tradition and policy in regard to Turkey. I appeal to an established tradition older, wiser, nobler far – a tradition not which

The Lobby of the House of Commons in 1886, caricatures from *Vanity Fair*. At this time Gladstone, having come to terms with Parnell, whose Home Rule party held the balance of power in the House, introduced his Home Rule Bill. The MPs in the central group, left to right: Mr Chamberlain (with monocle), Mr Parnell, Mr Gladstone, Lord Randolph Churchill, Lord Hartington.

145

Gladstone and his family at Hawarden. Back row, left to right: Stephen and his wife, Mary and Harry Drew, Herbert, Helen. Front row: Catherine, William and their grandchildren.

disregards British interests but which teaches you to seek the promotion of these interests in obeying the dictates of honour and justice.'

The Turkish crisis was settled without war, but there was no further question of retirement. Terrible on the rebound, Gladstone had come back to stay. The vital thing was now to pick the right electorate for his renewed career, for, curiously enough, despite his immense popularity, he had lifelong trouble in hanging on to his seat in the House. He lost Newcastle when he left the Tories, and Oxford when he ceased to support the established Church, and his last victory at Greenwich had been so close that he did not care to keep it. Finally, in Midlothian, in Scotland, Lord Rosebery offered him a solid base, and his campaign there, where he drew huge crowds, marked the beginning of modern politics in Britain.

It is small wonder that the Queen and the Conservatives thought him a demagogue when he appealed to thousands of workers packed into halls or market-places and implored them to consider 'whether, when all is said, there is not still a difference between right and wrong, even in the relations of states and the problems of empires'. Disraeli's imperialism must have seemed trumpery and tawdry when his rival struck this organ note:

Remember that the sanctity of life in the hill villages of Afghanistan, among the winter snows, is as inviolable in the eye of Almighty God as can be your own. Remember that He who has united you as human beings in the same flesh and blood has bound you by the law of mutual love; that that mutual love is not limited by the shores of this island, is not limited by the boundaries of Christian civilization; that it passes over the whole surface of the earth, embraces the meanest along with the greatest in its unmeasured scope.

On the eve of his seventieth birthday Gladstone wrote in his diary that he had been morally forced into the Midlothian campaign as 'a great and high election of God' and given special gifts of strength, 'especially in Scotland'. Ireland was to dominate his last two ministries (1886; 1892–4). He introduced his Home Rule Bill and lost it in the brief third reading and won it in the fourth and last, only to have it thrown out by the Lords. Oddly enough, Ireland was an exception, among Gladstone's great causes, in not having presented itself forcibly to his ocular vision. He went there only once in his life, for a visit of a few weeks. In this he resembled the Queen, who in the course of a sixty-three-year reign spent five weeks in Ireland and seven years in Scotland. But then the Irish problem was so forced on every Englishman of that time that personal inspection was not needed to stimulate his interest.

It is not my purpose to go into the complicated pros and cons of the long-dead issue of home rule, but in view of all that has happened in Ireland since the defeat of Gladstone's attempted solution to her agonizing problems, it is difficult to imagine that any rational being today would not conclude that at least he had been working in the right direction.

And that is where I come out: he always was. If a man is consistently high-minded, if he constantly puts his own interest down, if he is fair and conscientious and industrious, how far wrong can he go in political, or in international, questions? Even in the two issues where it seems to me that Gladstone was most clearly wrong: his opposition to divorce and to the exemption from income taxation for charities, our modern experience might furnish him with additional arguments. He had not only the most open mind of his era; he had perhaps the only open one. His ego seemed gigantic to his detractors because he was able to suppress it. They saw the struggle; they did not perceive the victory.

As J. R. Green, the historian, puts it, there may have been a truer wisdom in the simple humanism of Gladstone than in the purely political view of Disraeli.

Chapter Six

VICTORIA'S CHILDREN

When the Prince of Wales lay gravely ill of typhoid fever in December 1871, the Queen arrived at Sandringham to take charge of the sickbed and household. A great number of relatives came after her; the rooms were crowded, and arrangements were not easy. But the Queen, as always, was in complete control. Sir Henry Ponsonby wrote to his wife:

Yesterday Haig and I went out towards the garden by a side door when we were suddenly nearly carried away by a stampede of royalties, headed by the Duke of Cambridge and brought up by Leopold, going as fast as they could. We thought it was a mad bull. But they cried out: 'The Queen, the Queen', and we all dashed into the house again and waited behind the door till the road was clear.

As might be imagined, the awe of the royal family was not diminished by time. Here is how Marie of Roumania describes a childhood visit to the Queen:

The hush round Grandmamma's door was awe-inspiring, it was like approaching the mystery of some sanctuary.

Silent, soft-carpeted corridors led to Grandmamma's apartments which were somehow always approached from afar off, and those that led the way towards them, were they servant, lady or maid, talked in hushed voices and trod softly as though with felt soles.

One door after another opened noiselessly, it was like passing through the forecourts of a temple, before approaching the final mystery to which only the initiated had access.

Wonderful little old Grandmamma, who, though such a small, unimposing little woman to look at, should have known so extra-ordinarily how to inspire reverential fear. Our nurses would drive us along before them like a troop of well-behaved little geese, they too having suddenly become soft-tongued and even their scoldings were as words breathed through a flannel so that all sharpness was taken out of their voices of reproof.

When finally the door was opened, there sat Grandmamma not idol-like at all, not a bit frightening, smiling a kind little smile, almost as shy as us children, so that conversation was not very fluent on either side.

PREVIOUS PAGE A photograph taken at Windsor Castle in March 1862 shows Albert's five daughters lamenting their father's death. Left to right: Alice, Helena, Beatrice, Victoria, Louise.

None of the Queen's nine children, according to Queen Marie, ever achieved independence of her: 'Right into their ripe years her sons and daughters were in great awe of "dearest Mamma"; they avoided discussing her will, and her veto made them tremble. They spoke to her with bated breath, and even when not present she was never mentioned except with lowered voice.'

This relationship was well expressed in the famous cartoon of Max Beerbohm entitled: 'The rare, the rather awful visits of Albert Edward, Prince of Wales, to Windsor Castle', in which the heir apparent is shown standing in a corner, facing the wall like a naughty boy, while his august parent, with huge, drooping eyelids, sits silently contemplating nothing. For the children's problem was compounded by the fact that the Queen was not pressingly maternal. She was one of those women who gave all to her husband and had only a limited quantity of interest and affection to be divided among her offspring. At the time of her eldest daughter's engagement to Prince Frederick William of Prussia, she wrote a remarkably candid letter to his mother, Princess (later Queen and Empress) Augusta, a cold, critical woman who was nonetheless (inexplicably, to some of her biographers) one of the Queen's particular friends:

Queen Victoria sketching at Loch Laggan in September 1847 by Landseer.

151

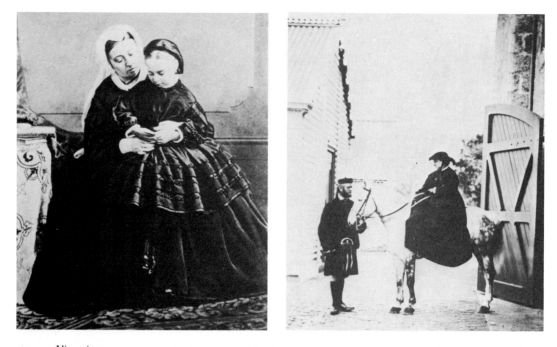

ABOVE Victoria was a devoted mother when her children were young, but experienced difficulties in communicating with them as they grew up. Here she is pictured with Princess Beatrice in 1863.

ABOVE RIGHT Victoria's children did not share their mother's liking for her gillie, John Brown, and resented her obvious preference for his company.

I find no especial pleasure or compensation in the company of the elder children ... Only very occasionally do I find intimate intercourse with them either agreeable or easy. You will not understand this, but it derives from various causes. Firstly, I am really only *à mon aise* and quite happy when Albert is with me; secondly, I am used to carrying on my many affairs quietly and alone; then, I grew up quite alone, always accustomed to the society of adult (and never with younger) people ...

The woman who could write of herself with such directness and insight was commendably honest but was obviously no easy parent for a shy child – and most of hers were just that. When the children were young, she was too concerned with their discipline and education to be as gentle as a mother should be. When they grew up, she became closer to them, but family duty was always a one-way street. It was limited to a question of what the children should be doing to help their poor burdened mother.

This failure of communication was particularly unfortunate in the first decade of the Queen's widowhood. All her adult children recognized the danger of her continued isolation and of her refusal to attend to ceremonies, but they had no idea how to convince her of this. It was once suggested among them that they should send the Queen a 'round robin' appeal, signed by all, begging her to appear more in public. It is just as well that this plan

Victoria did many sketches of her children and grandchildren. Here she has drawn two of Edward's children, Albert and Victoria.

was abandoned. The Queen would have disregarded it altogether, and any child who had persisted would have been roundly snubbed. Victoria could be very firm in separating herself from people who told her disagreeable things. Ponsonby's son Fritz relates in his memoirs how he was excluded for a whole year, while an equerry, from dining at the Queen's table because, after conducting an investigation invoked by herself, he had been unable to confirm the high birth boasted by her favourite Indian servant, the Munshi. It may shed light on her detestation of Gladstone that she was unable to keep him out of her way.

Of course, the children should have used subtler methods; they should have studied the techniques of Ponsonby and Disraeli. But they had been brought up as princes and princesses, not as courtiers, and they were incapable of indirectness. When faced with the need of asking the Queen to do something, either for her own good or for their own, they usually took their problem to an equerry or a lady-in-waiting or even to a minister to beg his or her intervention.

An interesting example of this timidity is to be found in their treatment of their mother's famous gillie, John Brown. That they detested him, one and all, seems sufficiently evident. They were appalled by his rough language to the Queen, and they deeply resented his familiarity with themselves. The Prince of Wales destroyed all his mother's statues of him after her death. But none of them, except the Duke of Edinburgh, ever dared to be pointedly rude to Brown. They knew, if the Queen had to choose between one of them and the adored gillie, which it would be.

Did they, particularly the sons, suspect something sexual in their mother's affection for the stalwart Scot? Was it a case of four Hamlets and a Claudius? This seems unlikely. If the Queen had harboured a guilty passion for Brown, would she, after his death and knowing that in scandal-loving circles she was called 'Mrs Brown', have seriously contemplated writing and publishing under her own name a biography of him? Much has been written on the hidden sexual aspects of this relationship. Let it be admitted at once that there is an element of sex in any love between two human beings. Brown was a very masculine man, and the Queen a very feminine woman. But that she should have admitted so candidly her tenderness for him points to the fact that she, at least, did not regard it as sexual. She loved Brown as a trusted servant, a person utterly devoted to herself, utterly sympathetic, a man whom she could *own*. He was like a growling bulldog that hates all the world but its own master. Who has not at times felt a desire for that kind of exclusive devotion? The Queen, after Brown's death, wrote to his brother Hugh in this remarkably intimate vein:

I found these words in an old Diary or Journal of mine. I was in great trouble about the Princess Royal who had lost her child in '66 and dear John said to me: 'I wish to take care of my dear good mistress till I die. You'll never have an honester servant.' I took and held his dear, kind hand and I said I hoped he might long be spared to comfort me and he answered, 'But we all must die.'

Afterwards my beloved John would say: 'You haven't a more devoted servant than Brown' – and oh! how I *felt* that!

Afterwards so often I told him no one loved him more than I did or had a better friend than me: and he answered 'Nor you – than me. No one loves you more.'

Did she ever love one of her children like that? One may doubt it. If Ponsonby was valuable because he toned down her minutes to officials, Brown's function was just the opposite. He expressed her formidable will in the corridors and antechambers of her palaces, to members of her family and household, in the rough, peremptory manner that she at heart intended. A railroad official, who received Brown's curt message that the royal train was jolting 'like the devil', complained about the 'coarse phonograph' thus used to transmit the Queen's 'gentle complaint'. But the phonograph and the complainer were more alike than he imagined.

The Queen's last Will and Testament expressed her trust that she would be reunited in death with her husband, her mother and the three children and three sons-in-law who had gone before her, but she also hoped to meet those who had faithfully and devotedly served her, 'especially good John Brown'.

The Queen's greatest domestic trouble, all of her own creation, was with her heir. There must have been moments when she envied the Roman emperors their right of choosing their successor within and sometimes without the imperial family. Whom would she have chosen? Probably her third son, Arthur. Her prejudice against her own sex (of whom she seems to have deemed herself a unique exception) would have barred the daughters from the throne. Yet the irony is that Albert Edward, or 'Bertie', as he was known, was to prove as Edward VII as successful a monarch as she herself.

There are, in the main, two prevailing views about Edward VII. There are those who regard him as the first gentleman of Europe in his day, the perfect diplomat, the conscientious and untiring constitutional monarch who used his perfect knowledge of forms and ceremonies to dignify the Empire and smooth the way to peace and domestic concord. Then there are those, like the novelist Henry James, to whom he was simply 'fat, vulgar, dreadful Edward', and the writer Christopher Sykes, who saw him as 'the Lord of London, with his inscrutable German eyes, his Tudor face, his gross pleasures'. Sykes wrote a devastating essay about an uncle and namesake of his, a rich bachelor who had ruined himself entertaining Edward, maintaining, for his princely master, a house in London which, when not used for merry dinner-parties and gambling, was probably a discreet royal *maison de passe*. The older Sykes used to submit, with a frozen impassivity that only more excited the 'Tudor' mirth, while the Prince, amid the yelps of his sycophantic entourage, would pour brandy over his head, burn his hand with a cigarette or shove him under the billiard table and poke him with a cue.

Both views are correct. Edward in public could be as grave and splendid as Edward in private could be mean and small. He was not a bad man. His private life may be regarded as the

A photograph of 'Bertie',
Prince of Wales, later
King Edward VII, taken
during the 1850s.

manifestation of his sense of injury and humiliation at having been a disappointment to both his parents. They could never get over their chagrin that the heir to Stockmar's divinely protected constitutional throne should be a youth of light morals and lighter tastes, a clothes-horse, an idler, a butterfly propelled by nothing stronger than boredom from one pleasure to another. Poor Bertie was made constantly to feel that he had let them down, let Britain down, let the Empire down. It started as far back as he could remember. When he was caught kissing a girl, in his teens, it was promptly reported to the Prince Consort, who sternly labelled the episode a 'little squalid debauch'. When Bertie, undaunted, graduated from kissing to an affair with an actress, he was made to feel that he had killed his father, whose final illness, most unfortunately, happened to coincide with his son's liaison. Yet had Bertie had to cope only with a strict and remorseless discipline, he might have come through it unscathed. The cruellest part of his upbringing was that he was forced to feel that his parents were motivated only by love and affection. It is bad enough to be kicked around by a despot, but most victims have at least the consolation of cherishing a sense of injury. This was torn away from Bertie. He felt himself not only incompetent and stupid but ungrateful and unloving. Even as an old man, it was said that his eyes would fill with tears in any discussion of his father.

What he did with his life was just about all that he could have done. He was given no proper employment by his mother in the six decades that had to elapse before he could succeed her, and he had only a light intellectual equipment. He used his social talents usefully for the monarchy in filling the ceremonial void created by his widowed mother's obstinate seclusion. Arthur Ponsonby describes his wonderful way with people:

It would be quite impossible to overestimate what amounted to genius. It is not too much to say that in spite of drawbacks, faults and failures, it *made* him. With a dignified presence, a fine profile (as his coins show) and a courtly manner, he never missed saying a word to the humblest visitor, attendant or obscure official. He would enter a room and, with the skill of an accomplished billiard-player, look forward several strokes ahead, so that no one was left out. The appropriate remark, the telling serious phrase and the amusing joke, accompanied by a gurgling laugh to the close friend, made all delighted even to watch him. Although he never mastered a state paper, he had a wonderful talent for picking up tags gathered from people in the know, as Sir

The Queen with Edward
and Alexandra. Victoria,
jealous of her own
power, would not allow
her son to bear any
responsibility in
government until the last
years of her reign.

Charles Dilke, who was intimate with him, noticed. So that foreign Ambassadors, Ministers of the Crown, representatives of the services and eminent men in all walks of life regarded him as the most accomplished Prince and later the best-informed monarch that ever reigned. But it was all *façade*, the most engaging, decorative but quite misleading *façade*. There was practically nothing behind.

It is sad that the Queen could never bring herself to give her son credit for his charm and diplomacy. But she couldn't. To her his life was nothing but idle, fashionable frivolity. She refused to see that he was really doing her job while she frittered away the days at her desk sticking her fingers in political pies that she would have done far better to leave alone. Or, just possibly, she *did* have moments of suspecting the true state of affairs. If so, it probably only made matters worse. It is amusing to note her jealousy of any public demonstration for the Prince and Princess of Wales. When she at last consented to drive out in the streets of London, three years after the Prince Consort's death, she recorded her reception in this smug entry in her journal: 'Everyone says that the difference shown when *I* appear, and when Bertie and Alix drive, is *not* to be described. Naturally for them no one stops or *runs* as they always did, and *do* doubly now for *me*.'

Bertie and his beautiful wife did their best to keep up the outward show of royalty, and for the most part they were successful. There were a couple of scandals, as when the Prince was involved in disciplining a card cheat and again as a witness in a divorce case, but considering the thousands of lavish parties that he attended, and the decades of gambling and hunting and sporting, and considering, too, the great number of his actual adulteries, he must, on the whole, have been remarkably discreet. Is it any wonder that he was constantly bored and occasionally petty, even cruel? When he at last succeeded to the throne, he observed that it was too late. He was old and ailing. But he made an excellent king, though constantly haunted by the sense that his ministers never took him as seriously as they had his mother. Why should they have? He was not always attacking their prerogatives.

In Victorian days, adultery was permissible if discreet. If the offended spouse took no umbrage, society felt no obligation to do so. The Princess of Wales behaved admirably about her husband's infidelities; so far as one can tell, she made no scenes but simply took occasional extended vacations with relatives on the Continent. The Prince and the Queen's second son, Alfred, Duke of Edinburgh, are supposed to have asked Lord Rosebery, while

Alfred, probably the most intelligent of Victoria's sons, succeeded his childless uncle in Coburg and died a year before his mother.

the latter was still a bachelor, for the use of his London house as a place to meet actresses. Lord Rosebery refused, but one has no doubt that other householders were found of greater compliance. Christopher Sykes would not have failed to oblige.

Alfred was probably the most intelligent of Victoria's sons, but he was of a dour and moody personality and seems not to have much attracted people. His name was frequently under consideration for empty or about-to-be-created thrones: Thuringia, Greece, Constantinople, and he was ultimately induced to give up the naval career that he loved in order to succeed his childless uncle, Ernest, the Prince Consort's older brother, as Duke of Saxe-Coburg-Gotha. Poor Alfred regarded Coburg as exile, and he was already afflicted with the illness that was to cause his death, a year before his mother's, when he took up his abode there. He had also the burden of thus becoming a subject of his obnoxious nephew, the Kaiser. He had married a Russian Grand Duchess who disliked England and resented a rank in the British

Court inferior to that which she had enjoyed in St Petersburg as the Czar's only daughter. So far as one can make out from the scanty references to him in the Queen's letters and journal, Alfred seems to have been the least close to her of her sons.

Arthur, Duke of Connaught, named for the Duke of Wellington, had a much more satisfactory career than his immediately older brother, for he was allowed to remain an army man, and a highly professional one, throughout a busy, useful and sunny life. He was the perfect junior royalty, efficient in his duties, smartly military in his bearing, patriotic, decorative, happily married. He became a symbol of the thin red line, a kind of one-man parade. One imagines him as constantly on horseback, reviewing troops, returning salutes, Kiplingesque, the role that used to be played by C. Aubrey Smith in films about the Empire. He was reputedly the Queen's favourite son, yet in 1867, when he was seventeen and coming to Osborne to see his mother after a long absence, Ponsonby notes: 'The Queen is an odd woman. I believe she is as fond of her children as anyone. Yet she was going out driving and started at 3.25. Just as she was getting in, up comes the advance Groom to say Arthur had arrived and was following, yet she wouldn't wait for one minute to receive him, and drove off.'

Leopold, the youngest son, suffered from haemophilia, a disease that was to turn up again and again in the descendants of three of his sisters. The Queen allowed him greater liberties with herself because of his illness and even made him a sort of under-secretary, but although gentle of manner and possessed of considerable charm and intelligence, he made matters difficult for the ministers because of his indiscretion. He died young, although not before he had married Princess Helena of Waldeck and sired two children, Prince Charles Edward and Princess Alice. The former was to succeed his uncle Alfred as Duke of Saxe-Coburg-Gotha. It may be noted here the Queen had the sadness of surviving three of her nine children and of knowing, when she herself was dying, that she would soon be followed by her eldest daughter, the Empress Frederick, born Victoria, Princess Royal.

The Empress was the most interesting of the Queen's children: she had the best brain and the strongest personality. Adored by her father and married at seventeen to the ultimate heir to the

Prussian throne, Frederick William, later Crown Prince and Emperor, she was sent off to Berlin to help carry out the dreams of Albert and Stockmar for a united Germany under a constitutional monarch. But the career that started so brightly was to end in failures and humiliations, many of which were brought on by herself.

The Crown Princess has become the classic example among royalties of the futility of brains without tact. She saw issues so clearly, and she felt them so strongly, that it was difficult for her to believe that others might not agree. Bismarck treated her brutally, but one can certainly understand, at least from his point of view, that she had to be kept out of action. Like her father, like Stockmar, she believed that the sovereign should be morally pure but also politically strong. One wonders, from the endless emphases of her endless correspondence, if there were not times when those of the opposing view wanted to hit her over the head. She was badly treated, yes, but she filled the mails of Europe with her complaints. She always knew just what should be done, and it was so clear, so simple, if only somebody would *listen*.

Her niece Marie of Roumania describes the luminous harmony between her aunt's radiant smile and remarkably blue eyes, but she goes on to add that the smile had a bite in it, what the Roumanians called 'sunshine with teeth'. The Crown Princess spoke English with a marked German accent, and one suspects that she may have allowed a flavour of her native isle to season her German. Her brother Bertie's often quoted remark that she was at her most British in Berlin and at her most Prussian in London is a precise explanation of the tragedy of her life. One develops a vivid picture of her through her correspondence; one visualizes her slapping her hands together, coming up with the *mot juste*, showing off her erudition, rather overwhelming her interlocutor, yet still warm. Disraeli described her to Lady Bradford: 'I sate at dinner next to the Crown Princess who took the opportunity of making one of her grandest displays: aesthetical, literary, philosophical.' If she could have only relaxed sometimes!

She managed to antagonize almost everybody. So long as Prussia was at peace with her neighbours, the Crown Princess was vehement in her criticism of her father-in-law's policy of aggression in foreign affairs and repression in domestic. She loudly proclaimed her dislike of Bismarck: she saw him as a devil incarnate who was going to turn her father's dream of a united, peace-loving Germany under a constitutional monarch into a

Vicky and Fritz pictured here in London in 1858. She carried her father's dreams and ambitions with her to Berlin only to see her hopes dashed one by one. She and her mother were faithful and prolific correspondents.

163

hideous nightmare of despotism. It is not clear to what extent she dominated her husband, but she certainly acted as a strong balance to any theories of absolutism that may have occasionally tempted him, as his father's only son and heir. The Crown Prince and Princess were ostracized in Court circles for their defence of a free press. Yet the moment war broke out, at the very first sound of the trumpet, the Crown Princess tossed liberalism to the dogs and became a fiery Brünnhilde.

Of course, it is only fair to remember that the Crown Prince always went straight to the front. A cause draped in her husband's banner and fought at the risk of his life must have seemed a far nobler thing than one strutting under the Iron Chancellor's obscene colours. When Prussia and Austria attacked Denmark to seize Schleswig-Holstein, and again when Prussia assaulted Austria and her allied German states, the Crown Princess's letters to her mother seemed almost to scream. Here is a sample:

I assure you that if the rest of Europe did but know the details of this war – the light in which our officers and men – and our public at large have shown themselves – the Prussian people would stand high in the eyes of everyone, and I feel that I am *now* every bit as proud of being a Prussian as I am of being an Englishwoman and that is saying a very great deal, as you know what a 'John Bull' I am and how enthusiastic about my home. I must say the Prussians are a superior race, as regards intelligence and humanity, education and kindheartedness – and therefore I hate the people all the more who by their ill-government and mismanagement, etc., rob the nation of the sympathies it ought to have. My affection to it is not blind – but sincere – for I respect and admire their valuable and sterling good qualities ...

You know I am not blind or prejudiced, but I must say I have the greatest respect and admiration for our soldiers. I think they behave wonderfully. I hope you will read some of our papers to have an idea of what they have gone through.

It was to be even worse in 1870. Victory had been sure from the beginning in the conflicts with Denmark and Austria, but when war came with France, the Crown Princess at first feared a licking. She was ready, however, to fight with her back to the wall: 'We have been shamefully forced into this war, and the feeling of indignation against an act of such crying injustice has risen in two days here to such a pitch that you would hardly believe it; there is a universal cry "To arms" to resist an enemy who so wantonly insults us.'

Queen Victoria with Vicky's son, the future Kaiser Wilhelm II. They remained devoted to each other.

When, instead of being pushed back to Berlin, the Crown Prince swept triumphantly into France, his wife became both exultant and smug. She sent gibes through her mother to the Prince and Princess of Wales who had been so anti-Prussian in the Schleswig-Holstein war: 'What will Bertie and Alix say to all these marvellous events!' While the French had exhausted themselves in debauch, according to the Crown Princess, the dull 'plodding, hardworking, serious life' of the Germans had made them strong. She wept crocodile tears over the fate of Gaul:

Such a downfall is a melancholy thing, but it is meant to teach deep lessons. May we all learn what frivolity, conceit and immorality lead to! The French people have trusted in their own excellence, have completely deceived themselves. Where is their army? Where are their statesmen? They despised and hated the Germans, whom they considered it quite lawful to insult. How they have been punished!

But did the Crown Princess get any credit for this jingoism in Berlin? None at all. No one there, after all, could read her letters to her mother. All they knew was that the Crown Prince, presumably at his wife's dictation, was opposing the bombardment of Paris. He was going to allow good German soldiers to die in a long siege because the hated Englishwoman sought to spare a few Gallic monuments! Even in London the Crown Princess's kind-hearted gestures were not appreciated. She wanted her mother to give to the Empress Eugénie, who had fled to exile in England, a screen which German soldiers had picked up in the Château of St Cloud. The Queen refused. In the first place, there was a question of title between the Empress Eugénie and the new Republican government of France. In the second, there was a question of tact. Why should the imperial refugee be grateful to receive her screen from the hands of a Prussian looter? The Crown Princess could do nothing right.

She had bad luck, it was true, but bad luck seems to haunt the tactless. When, thirty years after her marriage, her veteran father-in-law, Emperor Wilhelm I, died at the age of ninety, and her husband at last succeeded, he had cancer of the throat. His reign lasted only three months. It was too brief even for a change of ministry; the speechless, dying new monarch could only sign a request that Bismarck stay on. The Empress Frederick, as she now styled herself, a widow at forty-seven, saw Germany fall under the control of her son, the giddy Wilhelm II, who disliked and resented her. The final irony was that it was *he*, her own child, who finally dismissed the hated Bismarck, but that when he did so, she had come to regard the old Chancellor as the lesser of two evils!

One can concede that fate had stacked the cards against the Empress and still observe that she did not play her hand with any great skill. Bismarck was rough and rude, and he could be gross; in his ugly moods he respected neither rank nor sex, but he was always susceptible to the Empress's charm, and she could have used it to much greater effect. And with her son her ineptitude was inexcusable. Granted that Wilhelm II was vain, volatile and glory-lusting; he was also intelligent, affectionate and oddly fair. The Empress should have made more allowance for the humiliation to such a man, otherwise strong and handsome, of a withered arm. A little flattery, a little sympathy, above all a little demonstrative love, and 'Willie' might have been hers, as her three younger daughters were. But no, she could not bend. She had always to be right and to tell him so. He did not respect his father's memory; he did not respect her political insight; he did not do this; he did not do that; there was no end to it. Even Queen Victoria saw this.

The trouble was that the Empress expected people to be reasonable. She would not see that they had to be coaxed to be so. Had she been born, like her mother, a queen regnant, she might have been a great one. She was more intelligent than Queen Victoria, quicker and more understanding; had ministers of state had to make up to *her*, instead of the other way around, she might have been easier to live with.

It is fortunate that she was spared 1914. Had she lived thirteen more years, to the age of only seventy-three, she would have seen Germany and Britain at war. It might have broken her heart. But one cannot be absolutely sure. Once Willie and his sons had gone to the front, once the casualty lists had started to pour in, might the spirit of Brünnhilde not have reawakened? Might there not have been passionate letters, sent through the diplomatic pouches of neutral nations to her British sisters, protesting that Germans had hearts of gold, and asking why, oh *why*, could the British not see that the insidious French had made all this trouble between two natural allies?

One might have surmised that the Empress Frederick, so strong-minded, would have been the one child of Victoria's to have had an influence on her, but this does not seem to have been the case. The Queen was suspicious of strong-minded persons; she had to be, for they were always putting pressure on her. In

1877 she was content to allow 'Vicky' to echo her own indignation at Russian aggrandizement. Here is how the Crown Princess joined in her mother's military fervour:

How I do long for *one* good roar of the British Lion from the housetops and for the *thunder* of a British broadside! God knows I have seen *enough* of war, to know *how horrible*, how wicked, how shocking it is, and how *worse* than sinful those who *bring it on* without a reason, and plunge thousands into misery and despair! But are not *dignity*, *Honour*, and one's *reputation* things for which a nation, like an individual, must be ready to sacrifice *ease*, *wealth*, and even blood and life itself!

But when the Crown Princess, unconsciously propelled by Bismarck, who wanted to create tension between Britain and France in the Middle East, suggested to her mother that England should occupy Egypt, the Queen promptly showed the letter to Disraeli. His dry comment was that if the sovereign of England intended to undertake the government of Egypt, she did not require the suggestion or the permission of Prince Bismarck. The Queen, who quite agreed, told her daughter so, and in just these round terms. The Crown Princess, reproved, sank immediately into the submission characteristic of her siblings. 'I am very sorry I was so misunderstood about Egypt,' she hastily wrote. 'Of course I did not mean that ...'

The Queen was also quick to understand the danger that her daughter's children ran in being isolated from the rest of humanity by the Prussian caste system. This letter to the Empress shows Victoria at her most sensible and humane and helps one to see that in taking the lead over her adult children she did not have to rely wholly on her rank:

What I meant (but what I fear your position in Prussia, living always in a Palace with the idea of immense position of Kings and Princes, etc.) is that the Princes and Princesses should be thoroughly kind, *menschlich*, should not feel that they were of a different flesh and blood to the poor, the peasants and working classes and servants, and that going amongst them, as we always did and do, and as every respectable lady and gentleman does here – was of such immense benefit to the character of those who have to reign hereafter. To hear of their wants and troubles, to minister to them, to look after them and be kind to them (as you and your sisters were accustomed to be by good old Tilla) does immense good to the character of children and grown-up people. It is there that you learn lessons of kindness to one another, of patience, endurance and resignation which cannot be found

The marriage of Princess Alice to the Grand Duke of Hesse-Darmstadt took place in July 1862, soon after the death of Albert, in an atmosphere of deep gloom. Painting by G. H. Thomas.

elsewhere. The mere contact with soldiers *never* can do that, or rather the reverse, for they are bound to obey and no *independence of character* can be expected in the ranks.

Alice, the second daughter, also married into Germany, but less illustriously. She became Grand Duchess of Hesse-Darmstadt and helped her husband in the administration of a tiny Court in a small state with a quiet dignity and efficiency which made her as much loved as her older sister was disliked. She said once that royalty was an anachronism and might soon enough be swept away, but that as long as the job lasted one might as well do it properly. Had her daughter Alix, who became the last Czarina, possessed a fraction of her humility and good sense, she might not have ended her life in the cellar at Ekaterinburg. Alice had been close to the Prince Consort; she had been the one to hear from his lips that he was dying and to sustain her bereaved mother afterwards. She had the beautiful nature of one who is always being asked to pick up the pieces. There was something sad about her that makes her a creature of pathos. She died because she could not resist embracing a child who was ill with diphtheria. She suffered from the crises of faith that were taken so seriously by Victorians, and consulted David Frederick Strauss, a liberal thinker and the author of an unorthodox life of Jesus, but she seems to have recovered her religious serenity and died a believer.

Queen Victoria was now determined not to send any more daughters to Germany. If they were to marry mediatized princes, they could bring their husbands home. Princess Helena was allowed to engage herself to Prince Christian of Schleswig-Holstein only under this condition. It was hardly a brilliant match. Not only was the Prince penniless, dull, considerably older than his bride and obviously destined for baldness and wide girth; he had even been deprived of his commission in the Prussian army when his elder brother's duchy had been taken over by Bismarck. But he was royal and manly and had a pleasant disposition, and he was only too happy to settle down in England close to the Court so that his wife could be constantly available to her mother. Princess Christian, as Helena now styled herself, made herself useful in a long life of minor royal functions which she performed amiably and well. It was she who founded the Royal School of Needlework. Her husband, who had at first irritated the Queen by his complacent idleness ('Why don't he *do* something?' she was heard to remark, watching him from an upper window), was finally given employment as Ranger of Windsor Park where he was successful in using scientific methods to abate a plague of frogs. He even attained a mild diplomatic importance when the future Kaiser Wilhelm II married his niece.

If a minor, transplantable German prince was an eligible son-in-law for the sovereign, it was only a logical step to widen the class to include the British peerage. Why seek abroad to bring in royal paupers with gutteral accents when one had to hand the fine flower of the island's aristocracy? Surely a Campbell, a Marquis of Lorne, heir apparent to the Duke of Argyll, handsome, talented, rich and a political power in Scotland, was a more appropriate husband for the Princess Louise than some serene highness without even a castle to his name? All the Queen could do with Prince Christian was make him a ranger; Lorne she would appoint Governor General of Canada. Unfortunately, Louise did not take to her dashing husband as Helena did to her dull one, and the marriage was not only a failure but the only

one of the nine to produce no issue. A minor accident in Toronto was the excuse for Louise's absences in European spas.

The Duchess of Argyll, as Louise eventually became, was never close to her mother. She showed a flare of independence and a taste for mildly Bohemian company. For example, she was acquainted with George Eliot, a woman who shared a habitation, however respectably, with a man to whom she was not wedded. And then she was a sculptress, and smoked.

Last of the nine and last to die (I recall hearing of her death on the BBC when I was serving on an American LST in the Channel in 1944 – it made two ages touch) was Princess Beatrice. The Queen felt that she was entitled to the total services of at least one daughter, and she resolved to keep her 'baby' unmarried. This may seem horridly selfish to us, but we must remember that it was a common attitude of parents at the time. If a woman went through the pain of nine childbirths, she felt herself entitled to the life companionship of at least one of them. But the Queen seems to have carried matters rather far in her desire to guard the Princess from all possible temptation. One night at the Queen's dinner, Ponsonby announced that someone whom they all knew was engaged. Silence fell. He received a message afterwards that the question of marriage must never be mentioned in Princess Beatrice's presence.

ABOVE Victoria with Alice and her family. Alice had largely supported her mother in the years following Albert's death.

ABOVE LEFT Princess Helena married Prince Christian of Schleswig-Holstein who settled down in England as Ranger of Windsor Park.

OPPOSITE A photograph of Princess Beatrice taken around 1871. She eventually married Prince Henry of Battenburg on the condition that they should live in the palace with Victoria.

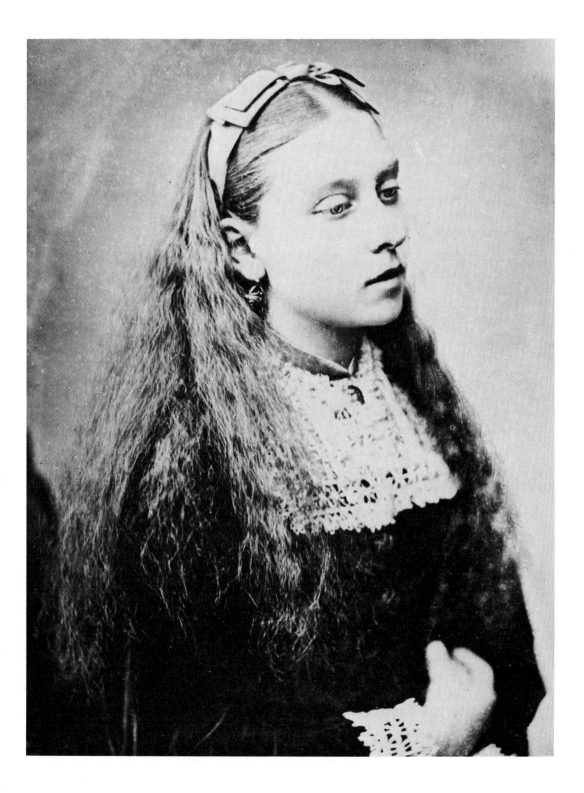

Love, however, as in the story-books, triumphed over the royal will, and the Queen was obliged to sanction her daughter's marriage to Prince Henry of Battenberg, a negligible prince and the issue of a morganatic marriage at that, but one whose brother was already married to a Hessian granddaughter of the Queen. The royal consent was obtained on tough conditions. 'Liko', as Prince Henry was known, had to make his home in the palace; he was not granted even the independence of the Ranger of Windsor Park. He accepted – what better position could he have hoped for? – and he became a model husband and son-in-law. In a belated search for some life of his own, after many years in the royal household, he requested permission to join his regi-

The Queen at breakfast in 1895 with Beatrice, Henry and their children. The Queen's Indian servants can be seen waiting at table.

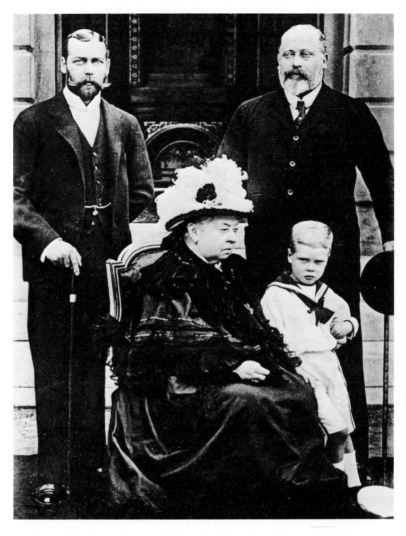

Four generations gathered together. The photograph was taken in 1894 at the White Lodge, Richmond Park, on the occasion of the baptism of Edward, eldest son of the future George V.

ment in the Ashanti war. Permission was granted – after all, he could not expect to take Beatrice *there* – and he died of an African fever on the way home.

Beatrice now devoted herself wholly to her mother. It was said that the filial side of her nature overshadowed the maternal and that she cared for the Queen noticeably more than for her own children. In the last years of the reign this kind of reverence became the dominant note of the little group of women who gathered around the Queen at Windsor, Osborne, Balmoral and Cimiez. Granddaughters had regular duty as well as daughters: Marie Louise and Helena Victoria of Schleswig-Holstein, Victoria of Wales, Victoria of Prussia; it was a high privilege as well

173

as a duty. Looking at the snapshots of these royal gatherings, on lawns, on terraces, in tents, with the huge hats, the dowdy, fussy dresses, the long equine Hanoverian faces, one can almost hear the gentle murmurs, the mild exclamations, the tempered laughter. I turn again to Marie of Roumania who remembered her grandmother 'surrounded by dogs, Indians, Highlanders, and also an aunt or two in nervous attendance or occasionally a curt-seying lady-in-waiting, in correct black, all smiles and with the mellowed voice usual to those who served or attended to the great little old lady'.

Beatrice, however, for all her mildness, was capable of one great act of vandalism. The Queen bequeathed to her the hundreds of little volumes of her private journal, and she exer-cised the discretion so entrusted to her by destroying a large por-tion of it. When one considers how passionately interesting are the surviving pieces, one can only weep at what has been lost. The Queen, quite simply, was a great journalist. She had all the qualifications: a sharp eye, a total recall, a searching curiosity, a capacity for strong reaction, an overdeveloped ego and a match-less grandstand seat for the panorama of history. Obviously, the deleted material must have contained all the most exciting family and political dramas with all the Queen's most strenuous comments. That this treasure-house should have been turned over to the tender mercies of a warped acolyte is one of the tragedies of literature.

But who is to blame but the Queen herself? Beatrice was what Victoria had made her. It is awesome to contemplate what the 'great little old lady' could do to those of her immediate circle. Victoria must always fascinate those who read about her. I have discovered that every book, good or bad, on Albert is dull and that every one, good or bad, on the Queen is alive. Her vitality is astonishing.

Turn her around in different lights. Now she is heavy, middle-class, censorious; now she is shrewd, worldly-wise, tolerant; now she is funny; now she is devoid of the least vestige of humour; now she is humble, human, deeply kind; now she is fiery, imperialistic, blood-thirsty; now she is generous; now she is mean; now she is politically astute; now she is reckless; now she is a hypochondriac; now she is full of vigour. The one constant seems to be her incomparable royal dignity; that never fails. She was always a queen and, I suppose, a great one. I am tempted to add 'in spite of herself'.

OPPOSITE Victoria and Beatrice in the sitting-room at Windsor Castle. After Henry's death, Beatrice devoted herself entirely to her mother, sometimes to the neglect of her own children.

Chapter Seven

LORD SALISBURY and
the End of the Reign

Anthony Trollope attended many sessions of the House of Commons to gather material for his parliamentary novels. The experience did little to reverse the unfavourable impression of parliamentarians already derived from his unsuccessful campaign for a seat in 1868. To Trollope the symbol of what was wrong with British politics was Disraeli, in whom he detected 'a feeling of stage properties, a smell of hair oil, an aspect of buhl, a remembrance of tailors'. He was speaking, it is true, of the novels, but one has little doubt, after the sketch of Mr Daubeny in *The Prime Minister*, that Trollope equated Disraeli the politician with Disraeli the novelist.

To keep his parliamentary series from sinking in the bog of his political pessimism, Trollope decided to create one great and noble statesman, a man who would stand high above the petty personalities and rivalries of party politics, a legislator devoid of vulgar personal ambition whose eye would always be fixed on the simple goal of what was best for the nation. So Plantagenet Palliser, 'Planty Pall', came into being, Chancellor of the Exchequer to begin with, and later as Duke of Omnium, to be Prime Minister.

Trollope seems to have felt that if he were going to endorse a fictional British politician with uncharacteristic virtues, he should at the same time delete all characteristic vices. So Planty Pall does not gamble; he barely drinks, and, once married, he never looks at another woman. He goes further; he carries his austerity even to innocent diversions: he will not ride to hounds (what this must have cost his creator!); and he is wilfully ignorant of all facts and customs of the turf and hunt. He has no gossip or small talk; he cares only for the Exchequer and a decimal coinage. In short, he is as dry as a haystack, and there is no greater proof of Trollope's genius than that he manages to make the haystack interesting.

Planty Pall is a Liberal, and he professes democratic ideals, but there is a contradiction deep in his heart. In all matters concerning himself and his family he is the darkest conservative. If he believes that all men are equal, he makes an exception for dukes and their children. If he believes in the brotherhood of nations, he distrusts 'foreigners' in his personal circle. If he believes in tolerance, it is not at the expense of a rigid personal conformity to social conventions. The real Planty Pall is an insular, puritanical snob.

Yet Trollope obviously expects us to share his admiration of his hero through thick and thin. When Palliser tells his wife that she must be less catholic in her entertaining, when he tells his daughter that she cannot marry a fine young man because he lacks a title, when he refuses to sanction his son's engagement to an American girl, even though she is beautiful, cultivated and rich, we are supposed to remain unshaken in our faith in his good character. For to Trollope the universe contained nothing finer than a British peer in full possession of his ancestral rights and properties, shouldering the burden of governing his social inferiors. He boasted in his autobiography that he had succeeded in creating 'a very noble gentleman, such a one as justifies to the nation the seeming anomaly of an hereditary peerage and primogeniture'.

Like his hero, Trollope professed himself a Liberal, but also like his hero he had basic Conservative reservations. In approaching his goal of equality among men, he admitted readily, he had no desire to travel too quickly. He was glad 'to be accompanied on his way by the repressive action of a conservative opponent'. It is not surprising, after this cautious platform, to discover that the nearest thing to his hero in contemporary British political life was a staunch and lifelong Conservative, Robert Cecil, third Marquess of Salisbury.

Let it be said at once that Lord Salisbury was never dull. On the contrary, he was almost excitingly interesting, whether in the bosom of his family or speaking in the House of Lords. His mind was quick and inquiring, and he took nothing for granted. Unlike Omnium, he put himself on a basis of equality in debates with his children and strongly fostered their intellectual independence, playing the Devil's advocate in arguments with them, even on topics as serious to himself as religious belief. He was sharp, witty, cynical, down to earth. But where he did resemble Trollope's hero was in his deep sense of public duty, his dedication to hard work at the expense of almost all diversion, his dislike of outdoor sport and his total indifference to gossip and social life. Lord Salisbury, most strangely for a politician,

179

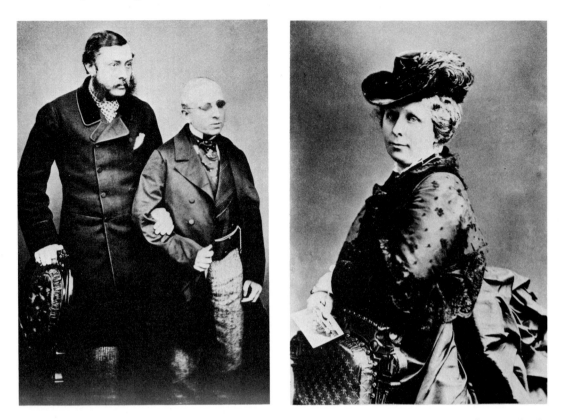

could never remember names or faces, and he exasperated his wife and children, returning to Hatfield House after a day in London, by mixing up all the social news that he had been commissioned to relay to them. Like Omnium, he had little personal ambition and detested even mild compliments. He preferred the quiet of his study to almost any contact with his fellow humans, and it is small wonder that his many years as the most public of political figures in the greatest of empires should have undermined his health.

His mother died when he was young, and his father, the second Marquess, was not a sympathetic parent. Lord Robert Cecil, as he was then known, was not the heir (his elder brother, the blind Lord Cranborne, did not die until Robert was thirty-five); it was questionable if he could even afford a political career, particularly after he had married Miss Georgina Alderson, a girl without a fortune. And then, too, he was of a moody, retiring disposition, and often subject to depressions; he had hated his schools and had few friends. It hardly seemed the start in life for a statesman.

ABOVE A photograph of Lady Salisbury taken in 1876. Her vitality and the domestic happiness she provided for her husband did much to help his political career.

ABOVE LEFT The blind Lord Cranborne, Cecil's elder brother, with his companion, Mr Johnson.

OPPOSITE Queen Victoria at a garden party at Buckingham Palace in 1897. Painting by Laurits Tuxen.

Yet the picture soon cleared, as it so often did with the Victorian privileged. He obtained a seat in the House of Commons through family influence, without serious opposition. His wife's vitality and flair with people made up for his own shyness and reticence. Domestic happiness rendered him more sociable.

And finally, he became the heir. By the time he succeeded to the title, in 1868, it was obvious to all that only Lord Beaconsfield stood between him and the leadership of the Conservative Party.

He seems never to have had any doubts about his political persuasion. It was not, certainly, that he derived much pleasure from being a marquess and a rich man; he cared nothing for pomp or sport, and he hated the London social world, which he contemptuously dubbed 'clubland'. But, like Omnium, he cherished the principle of aristocracy while despising the benefits. In hierarchy he saw stability; in the multitude, chaos and corruption. Conservatism to him was a cause to fight and die for; he deplored the lack of stomach for struggle in the comfortable classes. Their dread of the people, he scornfully asserted, raised what was often surrender to the dignity of a principle of action:

According to their teaching, nothing ought ever to be fought out. It is legitimate to show a bold front, and use brave language, and proclaim strong opinions in precise words; but it is equally legitimate, or rather it is a sacred duty, the moment that a determined resistance shows itself, practically to give these words the lie. It is hot-headed, it is dangerous, it is Quixotic, to terminate a Ministry, or imperil a party's prospects, or risk a single jolt in the progress of the administrative machine, in order to uphold deep convictions and to be true to a cherished cause. The desperate resistance which our fathers made to the last Reform Bill is blamed, not so much because their views were mistaken, as because it was madness to defend those views against so formidable an assault.

Lord Cranborne (as Salisbury was known after his brother's death and until his father's) was outraged when his own party, under the House leadership of Disraeli, introduced the Reform Act of 1867, which extended the suffrage even beyond what the Liberals had sought. He considered it a cheap political manœuvre designed to steal the thunder of the Left at the sacrifice of genuine conservative principles. He opposed the bill energetically and wrote a sharp retort to a friend who had warned him not to jeopardize his future leadership of the party:

OPPOSITE Robert, 3rd Marquess of Salisbury, by George Richmond R A.

PREVIOUS PAGES LEFT Victoria and Albert purchased Osborne House on the Isle of Wight in 1845, and rebuilt it in the style of an Italian villa.

RIGHT A miniature of Queen Victoria in old age. Painting by Bertha Müller from a portrait by Heinrich von Angeli.

185

Lord Robert Cecil in 1866, two years before he succeeded to his brother's title. He was at this time making his mark on the Conservative party.

I am trying to kill the Bill, or failing that to take the sting out of it: and I shall continue to take any opportunity that offers for contributing to that end. I do so because it is my duty to do so in respect to every Bill which in my opinion involves great danger to the State, so long as I sit in the House of Commons. The personal objects you urge upon me have, as I shall show you directly, no attraction for me. But if they had – if it were the dearest object of my ambition to become leader of the Conservative party – I cannot see how that wish could modify in the faintest degree my primary duty as a member of the House of Commons.

Obviously, the gulf between such a man and Disraeli must have then seemed unbridgeable. Cranborne made no bones of his contempt for a leader who was handing over the constituencies to the mob, or worse still, to the manipulators of the mob, to 'a class of men, not composed of those who enjoy wealth acquired by a long course of honourable industry, but of men who have suddenly acquired immense riches by some lucky stroke of speculation – men who have in their past lives given no guarantee that they will be useful and honourable members of this House.'

Disraeli was patient. When Cranborne avoided him at Hatfield, where Disraeli was visiting his father, the Conservative leader sought him out and embraced him, calling him 'my dear Robert' and making no mention of his offensive newspaper article, 'The Conservative Surrender', of which all the world was then talking. When Cranborne resigned from the Cabinet, where he had been Secretary of State for India, Disraeli (who privately compared him with a madman whose delusion it was to believe himself the one sane person in a world of lunatics) simply waited for the Reform Bill to pass and then promptly asked him to rejoin. Cranborne refused, telling Disraeli's emissary that he had the greatest respect for every member of the government but one, and that he did not consider his honour safe in the hands of that one.

Disraeli still did not give up. Five years later, when he started his second and triumphant ministry, he again offered the Indian job to Salisbury, who now accepted. For he was too shrewd and sensible a man to retire forever into the sterile corner of a petulant legitimism. He knew that if he was ever to accomplish anything in public life, it would be only through an even discredited Conservative party. A conscientious patriot had to be resigned to giving a leader as important as Disraeli a second chance. Granted that the latter had proved himself a slick opportunist in domestic affairs, should he not be given the benefit of a doubt in foreign relations?

When the Turkish crisis arose, however, Salisbury (as he now was known) suspected his chief of jingoism and sided with the pacific members of the Cabinet whose memories of the Crimean War inclined them to moderate any opposition to Russia. But when the Russians approached Constantinople, when there was an eyeball-to-eyeball confrontation between their army and the British Mediterranean fleet, Salisbury came over to the Prime Minister's side, and when he came, he came completely.

As Disraeli's Foreign Secretary, as his partner at the Congress of Berlin, Salisbury shared the burden and the honours of making the Middle Eastern settlement. Not only did he learn to respect his chief's vision in foreign affairs; he came to like him, aided in this respect, no doubt, by the ageing and ailing premier's increased dependence on him. Disraeli respected his younger friend both for his independence and for his loyalty. As he was later to tell Salisbury's daughter: 'Your father is the only man of real courage that it has ever been my lot to work with.'

A story to the credit of both men concerns the two vacancies in the Garter knighthoods in 1878. After the Berlin Congress the Queen offered one of these to Lord Beaconsfield, who said, very handsomely, that he could not accept it unless the other were offered to and accepted by Salisbury. Salisbury had no use for such honours and would have declined it, had not Beaconsfield's secretary, Montague Corry, come to him (presumably without the Prime Minister's knowledge) to warn him that it would break his chief's heart if he refused. Salisbury then had the magnanimity to accept.

Disraeli may have had some influence in softening the sharp edges of his colleague's conservatism. Certainly, the young Robert Cecil had started very far to the right. He had been against the principles of even the first Reform Bill. He had opposed the admission of Jews to Parliament. During the American Civil War he had passionately espoused the cause of the Southern planters. Indeed, as his daughter and biographer Lady Gwendolen Cecil describes it, this sympathy became almost irrational:

He refused to believe in the possibility of a Southern defeat. Even in '65 when, militarily speaking, the issue had already been for months decided – when an instinct similar to his own, dominant in Lee and in his heroic band of followers, was alone prolonging the conflict – he would not give up hope of their ultimate victory. Thus at each successive stage the bitterness of disillusion was added to that of defeat. There were moments when the nervous strain upon him became so great as to seriously alarm his wife for his health, if not for his reason. He took to walking in his sleep, and she used to recall her alarm when, on waking one night, she saw him standing at the wide-open window of a second-floor bedroom, fast asleep, but in a state of strong excitement and preparing to resist forcibly some dreamt-of intrusion of enemies – presumably Federal soldiers or revolutionary mob leaders. She recorded that never in her knowledge of him did he suffer from such extremes of depression and nervous misery as at that time.

Queen Victoria during Salisbury's premiership. The mutual respect that Queen Victoria and Lord Salisbury had for one another led to what was probably the most peaceful relationship between the Queen and any of her prime ministers.

The Queensland
Mounted Rifles
procession in the
Diamond Jubilee
celebrations, 22 June
1897.

In later life, according to Lady Gwendolen, his conversational allusions to the American Civil War gave no indication of the emotions which had moved him during the event. The world of foreign affairs, which Disraeli had opened to him, may have enlarged his vision to a scale where the slaveholders of the old South were seen in truer perspective.

When Gladstone broke up the Liberal party with his first abortive Home Rule Bill in 1886, the Queen not only sent for Lord Salisbury to form a government: she entered into active correspondence with some of the prominent Liberal Unionists (those who had opposed their chief on Home Rule), urging them, in the interests of the nation, to join Lord Salisbury's government or, failing this, at least not to oppose it in matters of national importance. She wrote to the Marquess of Hartington, congratulating him on his independent stand on Ireland and begging him to help a coalition 'so that the country (not to speak of herself) may not be perpetually exposed to changes of Government which upset everything and give a painful uncertainty both at home and abroad and paralyse our actions and policy'.

The Queen had been horrified by Gladstone's policies, domestic and international; she now decided that she must ally herself with the Conservatives, and for the rest of her reign she was to act as a sort of unofficial member of Tory Cabinets.

With Salisbury her relationship was different from that with any of her other prime ministers. Where Disraeli had flattered and Gladstone had stubbornly dictated, Salisbury was more of a friend, more of a business associate. Monarch and premier worked together in unprecedented harmony. Salisbury had a sincere respect not only for the Crown but for the woman who wore it, yet he was never dazzled or even much awed by her. The Cecils were accustomed to royalty. He had been a page at the Queen's coronation; his father had been her host at Hatfield. Three hundred years before, two of his ancestors had served as first ministers to the great Elizabeth. It was natural that cartoonists should depict Victoria in a ruff collar and Salisbury as Lord Burleigh.

But most importantly of all, both the Queen and Salisbury were convinced Conservatives, and neither had a personal axe to grind. To govern Britain and the Empire was for them essentially a job, a duty, not a thing to be puffed up about, not a thing to go to the head. One can see the great, thickset, rather weary statesman who might have been dreaming of his laboratory and library at Hatfield, and the stout little widow, whose heart was in the Highlands, conferring patiently, even laboriously, over Church appointments, over honours, over details of the forthcoming Jubilee. Salisbury was not going to flatter her; it was not in his character to flatter anybody, and as to opposing her when she took what he deemed a wrong position, what else could he do but present the arguments as logically and clearly as possible? He once said to his children that he could not understand anxiety about responsibility: so long as one had studied the facts and weighed the alternatives, a decision was a decision, whether it were the choice of an overcoat for a winter's walk or an order to the fleet which might result in war.

Such confidence was reassuring to the Queen, whose nature was full of worry. Knowing that Salisbury was a man of character, knowing that he believed in the prerogatives of the Crown and the peerage, and feeling, too, that he liked her, as a woman as well as a ruler, she was at her ease with him, as with no other statesman since Melbourne. She trusted him, as a man, as a peer, as a devout churchman. He had no ego, or very little – almost none for a politician. He was just the adviser that a poor, harassed, widowed sovereign needed.

When the Queen became unreasonable, Salisbury's technique was simple and effective. He would indicate, to begin with, that he shared her exasperation – which was often the case – and then he would calmly point out why she and he were helpless in the matter. It was this constant bracketing of their causes that made her see reason. For example, when the Queen, in 1886, fulminated over Russian superiority to British in the diplomatic battle, he wholeheartedly agreed. But what could either the sovereign or her first minister do about it? The Russians had unlimited funds for secret service; they could promote or discharge their diplomats at will, and they had a huge army. The British, on the other hand, were limited by Parliament to stingy sums, stultified by civil service, and had no soldiers on the Continent.

The Queen not only accepted this; she flew to the defence of her poor ham-strung minister. She quoted back to him his own brave statement: 'We must not lose heart, and do all we can' and urged him on in these ringing terms: '... and this is what we *must* do, and Lord Salisbury *will* succeed. Lord Beaconsfield raised up the position of Great Britain from '74 to '80 in a marvellous manner. Mr Gladstone and Lord Granville pulled it down again during the five years of their mischievous and fatal misrule, but already in seven months Lord Salisbury raised our position again.'

Could Disraeli have done better? Salisbury, like him, never made the mistake of minimizing matters that the Queen took seriously, but whereas Disraeli exulted in magnifying the royal concerns, Salisbury was more prosaic. He accepted the fact that once the Queen took an interest in an issue, that issue became important. This was not flattery on his part; it was simple realism. Should divorced ladies, for example, be admitted to one of the

A Downey close-up taken at Balmoral, 3 October 1896, when the first film was made of Royalty. From left to right: Francis Clark (gillie), the Duke of Connaught, Nicholas II, Patricia of Connaught, Queen Victoria, Princess Helena Victoria, the Czarina, the Duchess of Connaught, Margaret of Connaught.

Queen's Drawing-Rooms? She was very down on women who divorced, even with good cause, and Salisbury showed the skill of Ponsonby himself in bringing her around. He made the unexpected point in his memorandum to her that, as no decree could be granted in a divorce action if any conjugal infidelity were proved against the plaintiff, it had to follow that a woman who had divorced her husband had a 'special certificate of character'. Salisbury then proceeded to ally himself with the Queen's sentiments in a comment not strictly required by the question: 'With respect to *men* who have been divorced for their own adultery, Lord Salisbury would be very glad if Your Majesty should decide to give them no social recognition of any kind. It would have a very valuable effect on public morality. But this would be a very considerable change.' The last sentence ensured that nothing would be done. The Queen was delighted. She found the memorandum 'excellent' and directed Ponsonby to see that it was carried out, as to the ladies, adding the following: 'She entirely agrees about the gentlemen. It would have the best effect. Society is too bad *now*; some stop should be put to it.'

In 1889 the Queen was watching carefully to see which members of the House of Commons would be appointed to the committee which reported on proposed allowances to members

Queen Victoria writing, attended as usual by an Indian servant.

of her family. She was not pleased with the results: 'I am quite horrified to see the name of that horrible, lying Labouchère and of that rebel Parnell on the Committee for the Royal Grants. I protest vehemently against both.' Salisbury wrote back that the majority of the committee had been selected by the Conservatives and should be satisfactory to her. The minority, by custom, were selected by the other side. He argued that it might actually be better to have the radicals among these. They were bound to speak out, in any case, against the grants, and they might be hampered in their opposition by having served on the committee whose recommendations they attacked. Salisbury then concluded – thus again placing himself squarely on the Queen's side in the losing struggle of their century against vulgarity and greed – that there were no moderate Liberals left who placed issue over party. So why distinguish between them?

He did not, of course, always get his way. When he suggested that the visit to England of the recently widowed Empress Frederick might be deferred in view of the poor relations that existed between her and her son, Wilhelm II, the Queen brushed this aside. The Empress was her 'poor stricken daughter', and nobody was going to say that she could not visit her mother. 'Surrender', as she put it, would only encourage her grandson and Bismarck. 'You all seem frightened of them,' she wrote, 'which is not the way to make them better ... Please, let no one mention this again.' No one did.

Family matters, however, could not be left to the Queen when it was a question of appointing her son Arthur commander-in-chief in India. Salisbury opposed this, and for once he hurt her feelings bitterly. Yet she ended her angry letter on a forgiving note. She was sad, she wrote, to find her first minister

labouring still under the extraordinary delusion that the Queen wishes to *force* her son on, whereas it is the opinion of high military men who led her to believe ... that the Duke, *not* because he was her son, but from his fitness, would be the best appointment ... What is so offensive to the Queen is the sort of way in which Lord Salisbury treats the idea as so absurd and impossible. The Queen will not discuss it *with* him, she feels too grieved for that; and will not bear him any ill will for it, as she thinks he lets himself be overruled.

Nothing, after all, could be allowed to break up the team. In 1890, writing to express her sympathy at the annoyance caused to Salisbury by his dissenting colleagues, the Queen counselled him to

Lord Salisbury, seen here with Lady Gwendolen (his biographer) on his left, and Lady Robert Cecil.

bear patiently the humiliations of essential compromise. She then described their joint mission in these remarkable terms: 'We have to maintain order and the safety of the Empire, and imperial and national interests depend on the Gladstonians being kept from making even an abortive attempt to form a Government.'

Salisbury was the first of the Queen's prime ministers to be younger than she, and he was impressed by the rich political experience which she had gained in fifty years on the throne. As Lady Gwendolen Cecil put it, the Queen would discuss with him 'the characters and motives of the sovereigns and statesmen of Europe much in the same way that an intelligent and observant country gentleman's wife might discuss those of her country neighbours'. Salisbury believed that monarchy was indispensable to the Empire and that its continued credit was the only guarantee of national stability. As a young man he had been wont to say that he should have preferred service to a king than to a parliament. Victoria's 'inborn and inextinguishable consciousness of queenship' was innately sympathetic to him. He even tolerated her conviction that the welfare of the people was inalienably hers and that her ministers were merely stewards. To quote Lady Gwendolen again: 'This acute sense of responsibility, with the fundamentally self-devoted – if rather illogical – conception of her office by which it was inspired, commanded Lord Salisbury's unqualified respect, and he was quite ready to accept the re-actions of a less altruistic character that accompanied it.'

It is not surprising that the Queen, when asked if she did not regard Lord Beaconsfield as her greatest prime minister, should have replied: 'No, Lord Salisbury.' She had probably been fonder of the former, but Salisbury was her partner in rule. Understanding that honesty and sincerity were her principal characteristics, he recognized that the best method of presenting facts to her was honestly and sincerely. Ultimately they learned to protect each other with a rather fierce solicitude. The Queen was constantly concerned about Salisbury's health, and he would always jump to save her from anxiety. 'I will *not* have the Queen worried,' was his retort to colleagues who sought to press her to distasteful decisions. The words that she wrote to him after the fall of his first brief ministry in 1885 epitomize their relationship: 'The Queen does not trust herself to dwell on parting with Lord Salisbury. It would quite upset her – for the loss to her is so great, and she is *so* alone.'

Salisbury was prime minister briefly in the year 1885, again from 1886 to 1891, and, finally, from 1895 to 1902, the last ministry extending into the reign of Edward VII. The domestic scene during most of this very prosperous period was too quiet to take up the bulk of his attention, which was largely devoted to foreign affairs. There his constant goal was the preservation of peace, not so much by any international scheme as by day to day planning, adjustment and compromise. In somewhat the same fashion social legislation at home was slowly pushed. Salisbury was a Conservative, but he was also a humanitarian. He could always be counted on to support improvements of working-class housing and education. It was only mob rule that he feared.

His last ministry was the calm before the storm. The twentieth

Most of Lord Salisbury's attention was directed towards foreign affairs. The photograph shows a group of guests at Hatfield House, 9 July 1889. Front row, left to right: the Prince of Wales, Lady Salisbury, Lord Salisbury, the Shah of Persia, the Turkish Ambassador, the Princess of Wales.

century was forming: Russia, Germany, the United States and Japan were increasing alarmingly in strength, far beyond the dreams of those mid-Victorian diplomats who had seen the major threat to the European balance of power first in France and then in Russia. The scramble for colonies proceeded rapaciously. Salisbury never professed to be an imperialist, but he wanted England to have her fair share. A hundred million inhabitants and six hundred million square miles were added to the Empire while he was first minister. One seems to see him, a shrewd, wise, sceptical eighteenth-century man of reason, sighing at the prospect of world forces let loose that he knows can be only faintly manipulated.

Towards the end of the reign he became less of a party figure, more of a symbol of British predominance and common sense in a chaotic world. The tall, bulky, solid figure, with the great bald head and beard, was not so much associated now with Conservative politics as with the benevolence and wisdom that people wanted to see as the core of the imperial idea. Germany might have its screaming Kaiser; France, its shrill, pushing diplomats; but the serious, plodding old peer, dressed so casually as once to have been refused admission to the Casino in Monte Carlo, could be counted on to keep them under control. Lord David Cecil has vividly expressed the tragic irony behind his grandfather's career:

He died still a revered national figure with his party in power and his policies apparently successful: he had been Prime Minister of England at the Diamond Jubilee of 1897, which celebrated the highest point of dominion and glory ever attained by the English. In fact Fate, in a spirit of irony which my grandfather would have appreciated, if grimly, had designed these triumphs as though to provide a contrasting prelude to a period of spectacular catastrophe, which entailed, incidentally, the decline of most of what my grandfather had stood for: British greatness, aristocratic government, individual liberty and international peace. Within fifty years of his death, British greatness had dwindled, aristocratic government had disappeared, individual liberty had lost its prestige, and England had been involved in the two greatest wars in the history of mankind.

But one wonders if the smart old statesman did not at all times have a fairly accurate apprehension of the deluge that would follow him. He had always been a pessimist. He believed devoutly in God, but in a God who, for reasons unrevealed to man, allows events to take their natural course on our beleaguered planet. Nothing really mattered too much, Salisbury used to tell his children: one did one's best, that was all. I suspect that he understood that the sweep of international events in the last decade of the century was carrying Conservatives and Liberals, Home Rulers and Unionists, relentlessly along in its tide.

What about the morality, in a statesman who proclaimed so deep a reverence for human independence, of the grabbing of the African continent? Lady Gwendolen Cecil gives the answer that was accepted by so many of her father's generation:

But among the black men's rights it did not appear that he or those who worked beside or under him included, even in thought, a right to independence or sovereignty in their own country. The reason is not far to seek. That generation had contemporary knowledge of what 'Africa for the Africans' stood for before civilization entered – the dead, effortless degradation which it represented, broken only by interludes of blood-lust, slaughter, slavery and unspeakable suffering. It was impossible for them to feel doubt – far less scruple – as to replacing it, wherever occasion served, by white dominion.

And she ends her discussion of the issue with this exalted praise for the British officials who colonized Africa:

The rigour of their lives will seem as superfluous as it would be intolerable to a generation bred to a world of softer and lesser demands: imperialism in its stimulus as well as its opportunity was the root impulse of their political creed. But the ethic which governed their tutelage of the dependent peoples committed to their charge has assuredly nothing to fear from comparison with that of many later and more self-conscious champions of uncivilized humanity.

One doubts that her father would have been quite so sure.

As the Queen's long reign approached its end, her temper seems to have become more benign, matching itself to the rich calm of the great Victorian sunset. It is pleasant to read in the pages of Marie Mallet's letters of the placid household routine at Osborne and Balmoral and of the loving ministrations of the women who watched anxiously over the now always kindly old lady, reading aloud from the novels of F. Marion Crawford, arranging *tableaux vivants*, playing duets, sketching, fussing with Her Majesty's shawls on the long country drives.

There was sadness, too. The Queen's son Alfred died a year before her; Helena's son Christian Victor perished in Africa; the Empress Frederick developed cancer of the spine. The Queen,

more and more peacefully conscious of herself as a national symbol, would murmur: 'My people will feel for me.' She wept over the casualty lists in the Boer War, and, at the age of eighty, at the request of her ministers and in the interest of Anglo-Irish relations, she took the long, arduous trip to Dublin to show herself in potentially hostile streets.

Victoria's visit to Ireland was made in 1900, at the age of eighty. Here the Lord Mayor of Dublin presents the Keys of the City to the Queen.

There were no riots or ugly demonstrations, although the poetess Ethna Carberry, interpreting the royal visit as a recruiting expedition to send Ireland's sons to die in Africa, probably expressed the opinion of many when she wrote:

> O, Irish mothers, what seeks she now,
> Who comes with a smile on her aged face?
> The weight of years lies grim on her brow,
> She has almost run her race.

It seems a harsh description of the little old woman in black asleep in the victoria, awakened by the watchful equerry Fritz Ponsonby, who would spur his horse close alongside the carriage when he saw the royal head begin to nod.

In the winter of 1900 the Queen failed badly. Her eyesight was dimmed by cataracts; she was deafer; she could not sleep at night.

ABOVE Queen Victoria's funeral procession on its way from the Albert Memorial Chapel to the Mausoleum at Frogmore.

ABOVE RIGHT A rare photograph of Victoria smiling.

The end came early in January 1901 at Osborne, where she was surrounded by children and grandchildren. Pathetically, they called out their names to her as she sank into a final coma. For the last two hours her head was supported by the strong motionless arm of the Kaiser.

What was he thinking about during those uncomfortable hours? Was he thinking that it was fitting that the place of honour should be occupied by the beloved oldest grandson, a German like Albert, and not by any of the silly, mawkish English descendants bleating out their names like lost sheep? Did he picture himself, the warlord, the future arbiter of Europe, as the true heir of the dying sea-queen? Was not the imperial crown of the world passing from Victoria to Wilhelm? Or did he simply think, poor 'Willie', unbeloved of his own mother, distrusted by his English relatives, that he was losing in his kind old grandmamma the only person who could understand and still love him?

The police closed Osborne House off from the public until the Prime Minister had been informed. Then an unseemly mob of reporters rode their bicycles pell mell to the telephones of Cowes crying 'Queen dead! Queen dead!' The twentieth century had come.

BIBLIOGRAPHY

A. C. Benson, G. E. Buckle and Viscount Esher, eds, *Letters
of Queen Victoria*, 3 vols (Murray, London, 1907, 1925,
1932)

E. F. Benson, *Queen Victoria's Daughters* (Appleton Century,
New York, 1938)

Daphne Bennett, *King Without a Crown* (Lippincott,
Philadelphia, 1977)

Daphne Bennett, *Vicky, Princess Royal of England and
German Empress* (St Martin's Press, New York, 1971)

Robert Blake, *Disraeli* (Eyre & Spottiswoode, London, 1966)

Hector Bolitho, *Albert, Prince Consort* (Bobbs-Merrill, New
York, 1964)

G. E. Buckle and W. E. Monypenny, *Disraeli* (Macmillan,
New York, 1912)

Lord David Cecil, *The Cecils of Hatfield House* (Constable,
London, 1973)

Lord David Cecil, *Melbourne* (Constable, London, 1965)

Lady Gwendolen Cecil, *Life of Robert, Marquess of Salisbury*
(Hodder & Stoughton, London, 1921–32)

Frank B. Chancellor, *Prince Consort* (Dial Press, New York,
1931)

Pierre Crabites, *Victoria's Guardian Angel, A Study of Baron
Stockmar* (Dutton, New York, 1938)

Dormer Creston, *The Youthful Queen Victoria* (Putnam, New
York, 1952)

Tom Cullen, *The Empress Brown* (Houghton Mifflin, Boston,
1969)

David Duff, *Albert and Victoria* (Muller, London, 1972)

M. Walter Dunne, ed., *The Works of Benjamin Disraeli* (New
York, 1904)

Nina Epton, *Victoria and Her Daughters* (Norton, New York,
1971)

Viscount Esher, ed., *The Girlhood of Queen Victoria* (a
selection from Her Majesty's Diaries between the years of
1837–40) (Murray, London, 1912)

Frank Eyck, *The Prince Consort, A Political Biography* (Cedric Chivers, Bath, 1975)

C. R. L. Fletcher, *Mr Gladstone at Oxford* (Dutton, New York, 1908)

Roger Fulford, *Prince Consort* (Macmillan, London, 1949)

G. T. Garratt, *The Two Mr Gladstones* (Macmillan, New York, 1936)

Helmut and Alison Gernsheim, *Edward VII and Queen Alexandra* (Muller, London, 1962)

Helmut and Alison Gernsheim, *Victoria R* (Putnam, New York, 1959)

W. E. Gladstone, *Landmarks of Homeric Study* (Macmillan, London, 1890)

W. E. Gladstone, trans., *The Odes of Horace* (Scribner, New York, 1896)

Charles C. F. Greville, *The Greville Memoirs, Journal of the Reign of Queen Victoria, 1837–52* (Longman, London, 1885)

Charles Grey, *The Early Years of HRH the Prince Consort* (Harper & Row, New York, 1867)

Frank Hardie, *The Political Influence of Queen Victoria* (Frank Cass, London, 1963)

Mollie Hardwich, *Mrs Dizzy* (St Martin's Press, New York, 1972)

R. R. James, *Rosebery* (Weidenfeld & Nicolson, London, 1963)

Clare Jerrold, *The Early Court of Queen Victoria* (Putnam, New York, 1912)

Elizabeth Longford, *Queen Victoria, Born to Succeed* (Harper & Row, New York, 1964)

Philip Magnus, *Edward VII* (Murray, London, 1964)

Philip Magnus, *Gladstone* (Murray, London, 1954)

Victor Mallet, ed., *Life with Queen Victoria, Letters from Court 1887–1901* (Murray, London, 1968)

Marie, Queen of Roumania, *The Story of My Life* (Scribner, New York, 1934)

Theodore Martin, *Life of the Prince Consort* (Appleton Century, New York, 1875)

André Maurois, *La Vie de Disraeli* (Gallimard, Paris, 1927)

H. Miles, trans., *Disraeli: A Picture of the Victorian Age* (Bodley Head, London, 1962)

John Morley, *The Life of William Ewart Gladstone* (Macmillan, London, 1907)

Raymond Mortimer, ed., *Queen Victoria: Leaves from a Journal* (Deutsch, London, 1961)

Hoghland Van Norden, *The Original and Early Development of the Office of Private Secretary to the Sovereign*, doctorial thesis (Columbia University, 1952)

Hesketh Pearson, *Dizzy, Life of Disraeli* (White Lion Publishers, London, 1974)

Arthur Ponsonby, *Henry Ponsonby, His Life from His Letters* (Macmillan, New York, 1943)

Sir Frederick Ponsonby, ed., *Letters of the Empress Frederick* (Macmillan, London, 1929)

Sir Frederick Ponsonby, *Recollections of Three Reigns* (Dutton, New York, 1952)

Sir Frederick Ponsonby, *Sidelights on Queen Victoria* (Macmillan, London, 1930)

Magdalen Ponsonby, *A Lady-in-Waiting to Queen Victoria* (J. H. Sears, New York, 1927)

Jasper Ridley, *Lord Palmerston* (Constable, London, 1970)

Cecil Roth, *Benjamin Disraeli* (Philosophical Library, New York, 1952)

D. C. Somerville, *Disraeli and Gladstone* (George H. Doran, New York, 1926)

Ernest A. Stockmar, *Memoirs of Baron Stockmar* (Lee & Shepard, New York, 1873)

Lytton Strachey, *Queen Victoria* (Chatto & Windus, London 1921)

Helen and Marvin Swartz, eds, *Disraeli's Reminiscences* (Stein & Day, New York, 1975)

Christopher Sykes, *Four Studies in Loyalty* (William Sloane, New York, 1946)

Anthony Trollope, *Autobiography* (Oxford University Press, London, 1950)

Lionel Tollemache, *Talks with Mr Gladstone* (Longman, London, 1898)

Cecil Woodham-Smith, *Queen Victoria, Her Life and Times* (Hamish Hamilton, London, 1972)

Marquess of Zetland, ed., *The Letters of Disraeli to Lady Chesterfield and Lady Bradford* (Ernest Benn, London, 1932)

ACKNOWLEDGMENTS

The illustrations in this book appear by kind permission of the following museums, agencies and individuals. References to colour illustrations are printed in *italics*.

By gracious permission of Her Majesty the Queen 1, 8, 12, 16 right, 19, 24, 32–3, *41 below*, *42–3*, 44, 48, 49, 96, 109, *130–1*, 149, 151, 163, *181*, 200 left
Adele Auchincloss 125 below
Barnaby's Picture Library 60, 80, 90, 112, *132*
John Bethell *93*, *94 below*, *95*, *182*
British Museum 103, 141
Clwyd County Record Office 138, 146
St Deiniol's Library, Hawarden 120
Elliot & Fry 158–9
John Freeman 21, 73, 88, 153, 161, 173
Sir William Gladstone 125 above
Illustrated London News 55, 62, 116–17
Mansell Collection 38, 39, 45, 52, 55, 65, 67, 68, 74, 79 above, 86, 110, 111, 118, 127, *129*, 140, 145, 152 left, *164–5*, 170 left, 170 right, 172, 199, endpapers
National Portrait Gallery, *36*, *41 above*, 97, 100, *183*, 193, 200 right
National Trust *94 above*
Radio Times Hulton Picture Library 16 left, 17 left, 29, 57, 64, 79 below, 98, 156, 190, 192
Marquess of Salisbury 176, 180 left, 180 right, *184 (photograph by John Freeman)*, 186, 195, 196
Victoria and Albert Museum, Crown Copyright 10
Weidenfeld and Nicolson Archive 17 right, 71, 116–17, 134, 143, 146, 168, 171, 175, 189

Picture research by Marcia Fenwick and Miranda Ferguson
The author and publisher have taken all possible care to trace and acknowledge the sources of illustrations used in this book. If by chance we have made an incorrect attribution we will be pleased to correct it in future reprints, provided that we receive notification.

INDEX